World Cup 2007

World Cup 2007

The Official Account of England's World Cup Campaign

TEAM ENGLAND RUGBY

Copyright © Team England Rugby, 2007

The right of Team England to be identified as
the author of this work has been asserted by them in accordance with the
Copyright, Designs and Patents Act 1988.

First published in hardback in Great Britain in 2007 by
Orion Books
an imprint of the Orion Publishing Group Ltd
Orion House, 5 Upper St Martin's Lane,
London WC2H 9EA
An Hachette Livre UK Company

1 3 5 7 9 10 8 6 4 2

A CIP catalogue record for this book is available
from the British Library.

ISBN: 978 0 7528 9844 5

Designed in ITC Stone Serif by Geoff Green Book Design
Printed in Great Britain by Mackays of Chatham plc, Chatham, Kent

The Orion Publishing Group's policy is to use papers that are
natural, renewable and recyclable and made from wood grown in
sustainable forests. The logging and manufacturing processes are
expected to conform to the environmental regulations of the
country of origin.

Every effort has been made to fulfil requirements with regard to reproducing
copyright material. The author and publisher will be glad to rectify any
omissions at the earliest opportunity.

www.orionbooks.co.uk

Contents

Team England Rugby would like to thank Ian Stafford; Robert Kirby; Malcolm Edwards, Ian Marshall and Helen Richardson at Orion; Damian Hopley and Gaia Bursell at the Professional Rugby Players' Association (PRA) and the RFU.

Foreword

by Phil Vickery

Having both won and lost a Rugby World Cup final, I know which is the better experience of the two. So, although becoming world champions in 2003 is a memory that will obviously never leave me, I will look back on the 2007 campaign with at least as much fondness, if not more.

It wasn't just because I was captain, though to lead my country out on to a rugby pitch is just about the greatest honour I can imagine, especially at a World Cup. But it's not for this reason. Even now, when I sit at home in my armchair, stroke my dog and play with my little daughter, I look back at the events of September and October this year and realise that sport, like life, moves in very mysterious ways.

Nobody needed to tell the players just how bad a situation we were in after the second group game of the World Cup, when South Africa put 36 points past us, and we could not even score three in return. Back then, you would not have found anyone who would have predicted we would go on to reach the final and come so close to becoming the first nation ever to successfully defend their world title. Not even the players believed it. At least not immediately after that Springboks defeat.

Yet what happened over the next few weeks proves that you can achieve almost anything if you really put your mind to it. Even though we had started the World Cup poorly, I knew the squad consisted of a great set of rugby players, and an even more impressive bunch of characters. It was their refusal to lie down and die, their siege mentality when the world was writing them off, their willingness to address the problems that all of us – both players and coaches – had created, their bloody-mindedness, and their sheer bottle when the pressure was really on that saw us all through.

In the end, we are all massively disappointed not to finish the job, and that emotion, despite the incredible journey taken, will remain indelibly in mind. But this is not to dismiss the achievement of turning round what seemed a totally lost cause. After what happened in France, just about anything is possible.

The ultimate disappointment may be huge, but so too is my pride. I played alongside real warriors at the 2007 Rugby World Cup, and if I'm sorry we gave the English public some bad times early on, I'm equally delighted that we provided some enjoyment later on as well. As this book will remind us all, it was some rollercoaster ride, but one I'm so very glad to have taken.

Phil Vickery

Introduction

Date	Opposition	Venue	Competition	Score	Result
15 Feb 2004	Italy	Rome	Six Nations	9–50	W
21 Feb 2004	Scotland	Edinburgh	Six Nations	13–35	W
6 Mar 2004	Ireland	London	Six Nations	13–19	L
20 Mar 2004	Wales	London	Six Nations	31–21	W
27 Mar 2004	France	Paris	Six Nations	24–21	L
12 June 2004	New Zealand	Dunedin	Friendly	36–3	L
19 June 2004	New Zealand	Auckland	Friendly	36–12	L
26 June 2004	Australia	Brisbane	Friendly	51–15	L
13 Nov 2004	Canada	London	Friendly	70–0	W
20 Nov 2004	South Africa	London	Friendly	32–16	W
27 Nov 2004	Australia	London	Friendly	19–21	L
5 Feb 2005	Wales	Cardiff	Six Nations	11–9	L
13 Feb 2005	France	London	Six Nations	17–18	L
27 Feb 2005	Ireland	Dublin	Six Nations	19–13	L
12 Mar 2005	Italy	London	Six Nations	37–7	W
19 Mar 2005	Scotland	London	Six Nations	43–22	W
12 Nov 2005	Australia	London	Friendly	26–16	W
19 Nov 2005	New Zealand	London	Friendly	19–23	L
26 Nov 2005	Samoa	London	Friendly	40–3	W
4 Feb 2006	Wales	London	Six Nations	47–13	W
11 Feb 2006	Italy	Rome	Six Nations	16–31	W
25 Feb 2006	Scotland	Edinburgh	Six Nations	18–12	L
12 Mar 2006	France	Paris	Six Nations	31–6	L
18 Mar 2006	Ireland	London	Six Nations	24–28	L
11 June 2006	Australia	Sydney	Friendly	34–3	L
17 June 2006	Australia	Melbourne	Friendly	43–18	L
5 Nov 2006	New Zealand	London	Friendly	20–41	L
11 Nov 2006	Argentina	London	Friendly	18–25	L
18 Nov 2006	South Africa	London	Friendly	23–21	W
25 Nov 2006	South Africa	London	Friendly	14–25	L

3 Feb 2007	Scotland	London	Six Nations	42–20	W
10 Feb 2007	Italy	London	Six Nations	20–7	W
24 Feb 2007	Ireland	Dublin	Six Nations	43–13	L
11 Mar 2007	France	London	Six Nations	26–18	W
17 Mar 2007	Wales	Cardiff	Six Nations	27–18	L
26 May 2007	South Africa	Bloemfontein	Friendly	58–10	L
2 June 2007	South Africa	Pretoria	Friendly	55–22	L

England Record 2004–June 2007

Opponents	Played	Won	Lost
Six Nations	20	10	10
Tri–Nations	14	3	11
Other matches	3	2	1
2004	11	5	6
2005	8	4	4
2006	11	3	8
2007	7	3	4
Overall	37	15	22

As Clive Woodward was happy to admit in later years, all the planning in the run-up to the 2003 Rugby World Cup had been geared towards winning the tournament. Nobody had given a moment's consideration to what might happen afterwards. Well, what happened afterwards was the slow disintegration of the squad that had brought English sport its finest moment since winning football's World Cup back in 1966.

A spate of retirements and long-term injuries would prove a fatal blow to England's short-term results and would begin a difficult two or three years for the red rose as personnel, both in terms of players and management, came and went. The first to go was the best of the lot. Martin Johnson, predictably, announced his retirement from international rugby within a few weeks of hoisting the Webb Ellis Trophy high above his head on that wonderful night in Sydney. Arguably England's best ever captain, he was an impossible act to replace. Hot on his heels would come Jason Leonard, England's most experienced player ever with 114 caps to his name. In today's age of incredible physicality, it is highly unlikely another prop forward will ever reach three figures in Test match rugby again.

With two legends of the game departed, England lurched towards a RBS 6 Nations campaign in 2004 ill-prepared and decimated by injury. The rest of the world sat and watched incredulously as those free from injury were playing for their clubs one week after winning the World Cup. It was clear the strain, all released once the world title had been claimed, would now tell, and in the resulting Six Nations England, captained by Lawrence Dallaglio, slumped to a disappointing third place behind winners France.

Neil Back, dejected after being dropped by Woodward for the tournament, announced his retirement from international rugby, too, as did hooker Dorian West and scrum half Kyran Bracken.

3

Jonny Wilkinson could not even play in the Six Nations. Nobody knew it at the time but his career, save for a few brief appearances for Newcastle and, ironically, the British and Irish Lions, would be halted by a series of major injuries over the next three years, starting with his neck.

Just about the last thing England needed was a summer tour Down Under where they would face New Zealand, twice, and Australia. Jason Robinson was so mentally and physically tired that he asked to be left out of the tour. Ben Kay and Will Greenwood were told by Woodward that they needed a break, whether they liked it or not, while prop Phil Vickery, plus Iain Balshaw and Lewis Moody, were all suffering from long-term injuries.

Two of the World Cup heroes who did manage the trip to the Southern Hemisphere, Matt Dawson and Mike Tindall, would only just make it after both had been out for much of the remainder of the 2003-04 season with injuries as well. 'It's ridiculous,' commented Martin Johnson at the time. 'It's going to take our top players being burned out before people realise they can't place such demands on players.'

The June tour turned out to be disastrous. The All Blacks thumped England twice, 36-3 and 36-12, and then it became even worse in Australia when the Wallabies thrashed England 51-15.

Josh Lewsey, who had gone on to help Wasps win the Heineken Cup, was just about the last man standing from the World Cup-winning starting XV, but even he had run out of gas. 'You didn't need to be a brain surgeon to see that the guys were absolutely flogged by the summer,' he said.

Woodward, typically, held his hand up. 'I'm disappointed by the way I've handled the situation since we won the World Cup,' he said. 'I feel I've let down the players who helped win us the World Cup and have retired. I haven't handled their loss as well as I would have hoped.'

His dissatisfaction rumbled on throughout the summer as he

'I'm disappointed by the way I've handled the situation since we won the World Cup'

Clive Woodward

grew more and more frustrated with the interminable warfare between club and country. Eventually, exasperated by what he believed to be a complete lack of support for England's needs from either the clubs or the RFU, Woodward resigned on 1 September 2004. It would prove to be the second part of a huge double blow for English rugby because, just one day before, Dallaglio had announced his retirement from international rugby.

Woodward's assistant coach, Andy Robinson, was named as caretaker head coach for the forthcoming autumn internationals. The former Bath head coach took no time in naming Wilkinson, who had recovered from his first spate of injuries, as England's new captain. Robinson was also keen to stamp his authority, hence his decision to drop Dawson from the squad after the scrum half missed training to record an episode of TV's *A Question of Sport*.

Before the autumn series could begin, Wilkinson dropped out, injured again, and Jason Robinson was appointed captain. The first black man and former rugby league player ever to captain an England rugby union team, Robinson made an immediate impact by scoring a hat-trick as England humbled Canada 70-0. The following week, England beat South Africa 32-16 in a win inspired by stand off Charlie Hodgson, who helped himself to 27 points, which included a try, two conversions, five penalties and a drop goal. The autumn series would end, though, with a narrow home defeat to Australia by 19-21. Three second-half tries completed an impressive English comeback, but then a late Wallaby penalty won the day for the visitors. Still England, with Andy Robinson confirmed as head coach, entered the 2005 Six Nations with confidence.

Instead they fell at the first hurdle in Wales thanks to a last-gasp, long-range penalty from Gavin Henson. Wales's 11-9 win, with winger Shane Williams scoring the only try of the game, set them on course for a Grand Slam. England, for whom Matthew Tait made a debut best known for the way he was dump tackled by man of the match Henson, went on to see a 17-3 half-time lead at Twickenham a fortnight later against France disintegrate into a 17-18 defeat. A difficult trip to Dublin then resulted in a 19-13 reverse and, with Jason Robinson out injured, Martin Corry took over the captaincy. At least the 2005 Six Nations ended on a happier note, with substantial home wins over Italy and Scotland. Then, with Clive Woodward appointed as the head coach for the British and Lions tour that summer, all eyes turned to New Zealand.

By now Wilkinson had recovered from his neck, shoulder, bicep and knee injuries that had kept him out of Test rugby since his drop goal had won the World Cup back in 2003, and he was not prepared to heed people's advice that maybe he should ease off in the tackling department a little. 'I can tell you that if I did that I'd end up more injured than I am,' he responded. 'I'd rather stop playing the game completely than not play rugby in the way I've always played it. How could I live with myself if I didn't give it my all? I want to be the best and that's why I play like I do. So, no, I won't be changing my ways one bit.' Without him in the side, England had won just seven out of the sixteen internationals played since November 2003.

Some famous old English hands returned to Test match duty with the British and Irish Lions, including Dallaglio and Back, who had retired from England but not the Lions, and Richard Hill, who had been out of action with torn cruciate ligaments. They joined a whole host of fellow Englishmen but the tour proved disastrous. The Lions lost the Test series 3-0 against a rampant All Blacks, while both Dallaglio and Hill sustained further, long-term injuries. Wilkinson, too, returned home unable to play the game for a few weeks, although this would turn out to be the first of the next litany of injuries he would sustain.

While Trevor Woodman would soon be announcing his retirement from all rugby due to a neck and back injury that refused to heal, the game in England was boosted by the high-profile switch of codes by Andrew Farrell from rugby league to union. In a three-year, £700,000 deal funded jointly by the RFU and his new club, Saracens, Farrell was hoping to emulate his Wigan and Great Britain rugby league colleague, Jason Robinson, and become a dual international. The former Wigan and GB captain, with numerous trophies and individual awards to his name, Farrell was a massive coup for union, but he would go on to endure a whole first year out through injuries, as well as lost time as Saracens first played him as a flanker before he was switched to centre.

As England prepared for the 2005 autumn internationals, captain Martin Corry delivered a brutal assessment of what had taken place since winning the World Cup. 'Have we done the title of being the world champion justice?' he asked. 'The answer has to be a resounding no. I don't want to go into the next World Cup saying: "If things go our way we might win it." I want to go into the World Cup as hot favourites, just as we were in 2003, but that means we're going to have to win a hell of a lot of games between now and then. We've been world champions for two years and we haven't done the title justice. We haven't played like world champions so we've got two years to really make our mark.'

England had been smarting about that late home defeat to Australia in the 2004 autumn international for twelve months and, one year later, they exacted revenge thanks largely to a new star in the shape of a 6ft 5in, 18st 12lb prop called Andrew Sheridan. The man of the match in his first start for England, the Sale Shark's fearsome strength up front pummelled the Wallabies into submission. Wingers Ben Cohen and Mark Cueto scored the tries that mattered as England beat Australia 26-16, but there was no doubt that the front row of Sheridan, hooker Steve Thompson and tight-head Phil Vickery, the heaviest in history and weighing in at a third of a metric tonne between them, won the game for Andy Robinson's men.

The following week England faced the far more formidable challenge of a New Zealand side that had battered the Lions that summer. Although England lost 19-23, they finished the Test throwing attack after attack at the All Blacks line, who hung on grimly to their slender lead. At the end of the game the losers looked like winners, and the victors threw their muddied bodies on to the Twickenham turf with relief.

The autumn series ended with a hard-fought win over Samoa by 40-3, a game best remembered for the issuing of two red cards to Leicester team-mates Alesana Tuilagi and England flanker Lewis Moody, who became embroiled in a fight near the end of the game. Moody who, ironically, was trying to break up a spat between Tuilagi and Mark Cueto, became the first Englishman to be sent off at Twickenham. 'It's not something I want to be remembered for,' Moody admitted later.

As England looked towards the 2006 Six Nations they were boosted by Lawrence Dallaglio's surprise announcement that his experience with the Lions had rekindled his international fire and he was making himself available for England selection again, some fifteen months after retiring from the international game.

'I've got my personal life sorted out and I'm happy now,' he explained. 'You've got to remember I was part of the most success-ful England team of all time. Then I was involved with England at a bad time. I'm still very disappointed about the World Cup after-math. There was not enough done to keep the team together and we basked in our own glory and got what we deserved. After the Lions tour didn't work out for me I realised I'd missed sitting in that Twickenham dressing room, feeling shattered but filled with the warm glow of satisfaction that you and the team-mates sitting around you have given their all.'

Was there still a place for him in the England set-up? 'To be successful we need everyone to make themselves available,' he explained. 'In 2003 we had stiff competition for every place. Now England has competition in only one or two positions.

> ## 'I've got my personal life sorted out and I'm happy now'
>
> *Lawrence Dallaglio*

The guys need to know that if they don't perform they will suffer the consequences, as we did. Nothing short of winning the next Six Nations will do for us. If we want to take the right step towards the World Cup, England need to win the Six Nations. Andy Robinson has some big decisions to make. England have a Six Nations to play in, then a difficult summer tour to Australia, a hard set of autumn internationals, then another Six Nations tournament before the World Cup. Eighteen months is a long time in rugby.'

He found himself right back in the England squad for the first Six Nations encounter of the 2006 tournament, albeit as a substitute, as England took full revenge for their defeat in Cardiff the year before to thrash Wales 47-13. In a display that included six English tries to the one in response by Wales, Dallaglio came off the bench to replace captain Corry at No. 8 and score a trademark try from the base of a ruck. Lewis Moody also grabbed a try and ended the game relieved to be back after his sending off in England's last Test match, while Charlie Hodgson, looking good at fly half, kicked 13 points.

After two games, England were beginning to believe a Grand Slam might be on the cards. Although their 31-16 win in Rome over a gutsy Italian side was far from convincing – and the scoreline flattered England a little – it was still a more than useful win, and another confidence-boosting result. Mike Tindall, back from injury and reinstated in the England side, scored the try that broke the stubborn Italians, while Hodgson continued his rich vein of form with a try, four out of four conversions, and a penalty in a personal points haul of 16 points, with Mark Cueto and James Simpson-Daniel scoring the other two tries.

So far, so good, but all Grand Slam dreams were broken a fortnight later when England lost the Calcutta Cup at Murrayfield 18-12 after Scotland put up an impregnable, defensive wall that the visitors could not breach. Chris Paterson's five penalties, together with a drop goal from Dan Parks, did the damage, while England scored only four penalties through Hodgson. For the second time in three internationals, Dallaglio replaced Corry, which was seen by many to be a controversial, if not an undermining, experience for the captain.

Matters grew worse two weeks later when England produced a host of errors to gift France all three of their tries and an easy, 31-6 win in Paris, and a Six Nations tournament that promised so much, and started so well, ended in home defeat to Ireland, 24-28, to leave England in fourth place in the final table. Ireland won the Triple Crown and France, once more, were Six Nations champions. England produced a much better display against the Irish than they had the week before in Paris, scored a couple of tries through Jamie Noon and Steve Borthwick. But they were the victims of some highly dubious decisions, notably Shane Horgan's late, winning try when his foot appeared to cross the touchline, and the defeat spelt the beginning of the end for England's management team. Under-pressure head coach Andy Robinson was adamant he would be staying in his job unless told otherwise. 'I have total belief in my own ability and I'm not expecting to go anywhere,' he said. 'There is a fine line between winning and losing.'

The view from the RFU did not sound encouraging. 'The level of our performance in the Six Nations was unacceptable,' said chief executive Francis Baron. 'We're not doing it right. It's just not on to finish fourth.'

Sure enough, heads did roll, but not that of Andy Robinson. He survived the cull at Twickenham while his three lieutenants, backs coach Joe Lydon, defence coach Phil Larder and kicking coach Dave Alred, were all made redundant. For Larder and Alred, who had been part of Clive Woodward's management team when England won the World Cup, it was a sorry end to two sparkling international careers. Brian Ashton became the new attack coach, John Wells took over in charge of the forwards, Mike Ford became the new defence coach while Jon Callard took over the kicking duties.

They took charge almost instantly of a young, inexperienced squad, captained by the back row forward Pat Sanderson, to tour Australia while many of England's big names, including the previous captain, Martin Corry, were rested. The results, predictably, went the Wallabies' way as England were inflicted with two heavy defeats, although losing 43-18 in the second Test in Melbourne was a definite improvement on their 76-0 reverse when last touring Down Under with a similarly inexperienced squad, back in 1998 during the Tour of Hell.

In August 2006, Rob Andrew beat off opposition including Clive Woodward to become the RFU's new elite director of rugby, appointed by a four-man panel consisting of Baron, RFU chairman Martyn Thomas, plus two former England captains, Bill Beaumont and John Spencer. His job was to liaise with the clubs and produce a better working platform for England to operate in.

One of the first statements Andrew made was to declare head coach Andy Robinson's job as safe, but nobody was convinced, especially with a tough, four-Test autumn international series lying ahead of England. First up was New Zealand in an extra international to mark the opening of at least part of the new stand at Twickenham. With just ten months remaining before the start of the 2007 World Cup, it was an important game for both sides. For World Cup favourites New Zealand it was crucial to travel over to the Northern Hemisphere and flex their muscles, just as England went down to the south prior to the 2003 World Cup in Australia. For England they had to get back to winning habits, and fast, having lost their last five previous games in the Six Nations and on tour Down Under.

The good news was that an ambitious England threw everything they had at the All Blacks and hit them with a brand of exciting rugby that produced three tries for Jamie Noon, Ben Cohen and an intercept for Shaun Perry. The bad news was that New Zealand responded with four of their own as they romped to a 20-41 victory on Bonfire Night.

Losing at home to the Tri Nations champions was not the biggest disgrace in the world but, six days later, England left the field to the sound of jeers and boos after losing 18-25 to Argentina, and deservedly so. The Pumas were no mugs, of course, but in November 2006, they were ranked eighth in the world and had never before won at headquarters. The only bright spots on an otherwise thoroughly miserable afternoon were two wonderful tries by Paul Sackey and Iain Balshaw but, either side of them, Argentina went about their business impressively, with Federico Todeschini coming off the bench to wreak havoc with his boot and also with his hands, catching an intended pass from Toby Flood to Anthony Allen and running 70 metres to score.

A defiant Andy Robinson took a lot of flak for this latest setback, a seventh successive defeat marred by the kind of vocal disquiet rarely witnessed at Twickenham, but he still insisted he was the best man for the job as England looked forward to receiving South Africa the following week.

'I am in charge of the England team and I will be preparing for the South Africa game as usual,' he insisted afterwards. He did admit to this defeat hitting him hard, however. 'This is the lowest point of my career,' he added. 'I can only apologise to the magnificent crowd at Twickenham and to the country as a whole. We let them all down today.'

> ## 'This is the lowest point of my career'
>
> *Andy Robinson*

Respite appeared to be on hand seven days later when England, at last, pulled off a win at the expense of the Springboks, coming from behind to win 23-21 with a late Phil Vickery try and an Andy Goode conversion proving to be the winning scores, although it also took a magnificent tackle by Josh Lewsey earlier to prevent Jean de Villiers from scoring a try. At one stage during the second half England found themselves 12 points, and two tries, down, but a simple touchdown from Mark Cueto, a Goode penalty and then that Vickery try won the day for England who had now beaten South Africa on seven successive occasions.

The relief was evident afterwards. 'It's what we all needed,' said Andy Robinson. 'Credit to captain Martin Corry, and to all my management team. We stuck together in very testing times and we kept our nerve.' His sentiments were echoed by Corry. 'I feel incredible relief,' he admitted. 'But it will count for nothing if we don't succeed next week.'

Corry's words proved prophetic in the second Test against South Africa played at Twickenham, and the fourth and final autumn international. This time there were no stirring comebacks, only more boos and jeers from a Twickenham crowd that had run out of patience with a team that lost an eighth Test match in the last nine, this time by 14-25 to a severely under-strength South Africa. It started well enough for England, thanks largely to a Mark Cueto try that was lucky to be given after the wing failed to keep hold of the ball as he dived over, racing to a 14-3 lead, but they failed to score again for the remaining fifty minutes of the game, and saw their promising lead overtaken just before half time after prop C.J.Van der Linde powered over. After that the Springboks eased away with Andre Pretorius starring with four drop goals.

It was a result that, ironically, would save South African head coach Jake White's job, having been given a vote of no confidence back home. It was, however, a result that did for England head coach Andy Robinson, although he still refused to accept the inevitable afterwards.

'I'm not walking away from this,' he insisted that night. 'People will have their opinions and they'll be voiced, but I believe in both myself and this team's ability. The players and the management team have given one hundred and twenty per cent to the cause but I accept that any defeat, let alone three, is unacceptable.'

Martin Corry tried in vain to stick up for Robinson. 'This is very difficult to take,' he said. 'We're all under a great deal of pressure but it's unfair to blame one man.'

Maybe it was, but with the Six Nations starting in just ten weeks' time, and the World Cup in less than ten months, the RFU review came to the sorry conclusion that Robinson had to go.

'I understand the crowd's disappointment'

Phil Vickery

Phil Vickery's chances of even playing again had been largely written off after his back and neck were virtually shot to pieces, but here he was back again in an England jersey, and the Wasps prop was quick to launch an impassioned plea both to the England fans and players.

'I understand the crowd's disappointment,' he argued. 'They paid good, hard-earned money and England were just not good enough. But now is not the time to desert us. Now is the time to support us even more. Nobody hurts more than the players, believe me. I'm not bleating about the fans. They've been magnificent in the past and we've let them down. But we have Scotland in the Calcutta Cup in the first game of the Six Nations at Twickenham and we're going to need the atmosphere to be really buzzing. As for the players, I want the England team to get angry, to show it means everything to them. There is never a bad time to play for England. It's the greatest honour an Englishman can have.'

It was stirring stuff, and it was noted. Brian Ashton was promoted from attack coach to head coach and one of his first deeds was to appoint Vickery as his World Cup captain. It was a job the Cornishman had held before twice, leading an under-strength

England to victory over Argentina in Buenos Aires in 2002, and then a stronger English outfit in a 2003 World Cup pool thrashing of Uruguay. Clive Woodward has always maintained that the win over the Pumas was one of the great results under his reign, and helped set England on their course to eventual World Cup glory.

Ashton, too, deserved his chance. A former scrum half that once made it to the England bench but never won a cap, the Leigh-born rugby league fan had played union in Italy and France, as well as for Fylde and Orrell, before becoming one of the most enlightened coaches in the game. A stint as Irish national coach did not work out due to politics and personality clashes, but under his stewardship as backs coach the Woodward England team played its most attacking style until Ashton resigned due to personal matters. Work at the RFU academy followed, then a short spell back at Bath where, earlier, he and Jack Rowell had worked so well together to coach the best team in the country between 1985 and 1995, before he was called up to assist Robinson with England. Now he had the main job and, as from January, just eight months to turn a faltering England round enough for them to have a chance of launching a credible defence of their world title.

A lucky coach is better than a good coach, and at first Ashton received the kind of good news Robinson would have prayed for. Jonny Wilkinson was at long last fit and available to play for England for the first time since sending that drop goal between the posts to win the 2003 World Cup final. Since then he had suffered seven major injuries which had forced him to miss thirty consecutive Test matches but, after just a forty-five-minute comeback the previous week for Newcastle, he returned to the centre stage with an amazing haul of 27 points, a Calcutta Cup record, and a full house of scores – a try, five penalties, a drop goal and two conversions – as England romped to a 42-20 victory over Scotland. They made harder work of it the following week, seeing off an obdurate Italy at Twickenham by 20-7, and then came crashing back down to earth at an emotional and highly charged

'We were stuffed'

Brian Ashton

Croke Park in Dublin, where an inspired Ireland inflicted a heavy, 43-13 defeat on Ashton's men. The head coach was not one to mince his words. 'We were stuffed,' said Ashton. 'We were completely out-played by a far superior side.'

With Phil Vickery injured, Mike Catt took over the captaincy and helped his side bounce back to beat France 26-18 at Twickenham, with young guns Toby Flood, who scored one of the two tries, and then his replacement, Shane Geraghty, both shining.

What would have been a highly satisfactory Six Nations campaign – save for that blip in Dublin – ended on a low note, however, with defeat in Cardiff where Wales, led by a dominant pack and the mercurial skills of their new, young star James Hook, beat England by 27-18. England went into the game with an outside, mathematical chance of becoming Six Nations champions, but ended it finishing third in the table.

Steve Thompson, the England hooker during the 2003 World Cup campaign, had been on the verge of a recall for the Scotland game until a neck injury forced him to withdraw. In April the Northampton player announced his retirement from the game as a result of the injury and, shortly after that, Mike Tindall, who scored England's other try against the French, broke his leg playing for Gloucester at Newcastle.

It got worse for England, much worse, when a depleted squad, minus all their Leicester and Wasps players, who were facing each other in the Heineken Cup final, and Bath players, needed for the European Challenge Cup final, landed in South Africa for a two-Test tour at the end of May. In the first Test in Bloemfontein, England, wrecked by illness and injury, slumped to a 58-10 defeat, their heaviest loss ever against the Springboks. Much of the England camp had been ravaged by a virus – David Strettle being forced to spend time in a hospital on an intravenous drip – and even on the day of the game Toby Flood replaced Andy Farrell, and Andy Gomarsall was forced to stand in for Peter Richards. It was better the following week in Pretoria, at least for a while. At halftime England led 19-17 and were still level with fifty-three minutes played, but, after that, South Africa took full control as England ran out of gas, scoring eight tries in total as they thrashed the visitors 55-22. Although the England team likely to be facing the Springboks in their crucial World Cup pool game in Paris the following September would be vastly different from this, largely second-string outfit, it still presented South Africa with a massive confidence boost.

The next task for the squad, now replenished by the returning players from new European champions Wasps, defeated finalists Leicester plus Bath, was to head out to Portugal for the World Cup training camp. Many of the England squad members smelled a rat when they were asked to travel down to Southampton in order to fly to the Algarve. 'Why go to Southampton when we could have flown from London?' Ben Kay wondered. 'Then, when we arrived at the airport, we were told the plane had been cancelled and we were to stay in a nearby hotel. That hotel turned out to be an army base at Poole.'

It turned out to be no ordinary army base, either. The England squad found themselves at the home of the Royal Marines, and they were about to discover how hard these boys train. All luxury items were removed from the players and army kit was provided. Then, having slept in a large dormitory, they were woken up at 5.30 a.m. to start the day's training. 'The first thing I remember was how the rain was coming down in sheets,' Kay recalled. 'Getting wet, or rather absolutely drenched, would become a recurring theme.'

Indeed it would. England were there for only three days but according to most of the players it felt like three years. During this time they were pushed to their physical and mental limits. Exercises included being capsized in a canoe in the sea, going on long runs and walks carrying full jerry cans, jumping in and out of inflatable ribs at sea, racing each other in these ribs using oars, and carrying two-man canoes across sand for two miles. The first night's sleep may have been in a dormitory but, thereafter, the nights were spent outside in a tent. 'It rained, and our tent leaked,' was Kay's other indelible memory of his time in Poole.

Was it all worth it, though? 'Absolutely, yes,' was Kay's unequivocal reply. 'One of the main purposes was to discover the real leaders in the squad. We had so much respect for the marines at Poole that we'd do anything they'd tell us to. To my mind what was an even better outcome from our time there was how the squad bonded so well together. The way we responded to times of adversity then would put us in good stead for later in the World Cup.'

Finally, and belatedly, the players made their way to Vilamoura in Portugal where, for ten days, they worked on skills, moves and, in particular, fitness and fitness testing. 'There was one test where we had to sprint five metres, then drop to the floor, then jump up and run ten metres, then drop to the floor, then go to twenty metres and do the same thing,' Kay explained. 'That would be one rep, and we'd be asked to do one rep, then two reps, then three reps, then four reps and so on. The exercise only lasted seven minutes but I can assure you it's the worst pain of your life. I was left with a bloody taste in my mouth.'

After all this, it was no wonder the players were allowed the last night off for a blow-out. Even then, Kay was embarrassed: 'Mike Catt, Kevin Yates and I were just coming in from the night out,' he admitted. 'It was around eight o'clock in the morning. As we staggered into the hotel we bumped into Jonny [Wilkinson] who was on his way out for some kicking practice. To say we were embarrassed is putting it mildly. We all looked down at our feet and mumbled: "Morning, Jonny."'

Still, everyone returned to the England squad base at Bath fit and relaxed. From then on the fitness work was tapered down and they got back to working hard on their rugby. And so to the final build-up to France 2007. First there would be a couple of cuts in the England squad until there were thirty-six men left standing, and praying, that they would make the final selection for the England World Cup thirty to travel to France. Much would now depend on the three warm-up games in August, starting with the Welsh at Twickenham.

Chapter 1: The Warm-Up Games

Saturday 4 August at Twickenham, London

ENGLAND 62		WALES 5
Tait	15	Byrne
Strettle	14	A.Brew
Hipkiss	13	Shanklin
Farrell	12	G.Thomas (Captain)
Robinson	11	D.James
Wilkinson	10	Sweeney
Perry	9	Cooper
Sheridan	1	I.Thomas
Regan	2	Bennett
(Captain) Vickery	3	Horsman
Shaw	4	W.James
Borthwick	5	Sidoli
Corry	6	A.W.Jones
Worsley	7	Charvis
Easter	8	Owen

England replacements: Chuter, Stevens, Moody, Dallaglio, Gomarsall, Flood
Wales replacements: Jenkins, R.Thomas, T.R.Thomas, Popham, Phillips, Hook, T.James

Scorers

Tries: Easter (4), Borthwick,
Perry, Dallaglio, Robinson, Tait
Conversions: Wilkinson (7)
Penalty: Wilkinson (1)

Try: D.James

21

Saturday 11 August at Twickenham, London

ENGLAND 15		FRANCE 21
Abendanon	15	Poitrenaud
Sackey	14	Clerc
Noon	13	Marty
(Captain) Catt	12	Jauzion
Lewsey	11	Rougerie
Barkley	10	Skrela
Perry	9	Mignoni
Sheridan	1	Milloud
Regan	2	Ibanez (Captain)
Stevens	3	Poux
Shaw	4	Pelous
Kay	5	Thion
Haskell	6	Betsen
Worsley	7	Martin
Dallaglio	8	Bonnaire

England replacements: Mears, Vickery, Corry, Borthwick, Gomarsall, Wilkinson, Cipriani
France replacements: Szarzewski, Mas, Chabal, Nyanga, Elissalde, Michalak, Heymans

Scorers

Penalties: Barkley (4)
Drop goal: Gomarsall

Tries: Pelous, Chabal
Conversion: Elissalde
Penalties: Skrela (2), Elissalde

Saturday 18 August at Stade Vélodrome, Marseille

ENGLAND 9		FRANCE 22
Cueto	15	Poitrenaud
Lewsey	14	Heymans
Hipkiss	13	Traille
Farrell	12	Jauzion
Robinson	11	Dominici
Wilkinson	10	Michalak
Perry	9	Elissalde
Freshwater	1	Milloud
Regan	2	Ibanez (Captain)
(Captain) Vickery	3	Poux
Shaw	4	Pelous
Borthwick	5	Thion
Corry	6	Nyanga
Rees	7	Dusautoir
Easter	8	Harinordoquy

England replacements: Mears, Stevens, Worsley, Dallaglio, Gomarsall, Barkley, Sackey
France replacements: Bruno, Mas, Nallet, Bonnaire, Mignoni, Skrela, Rougerie

Scorers

Penalties: Wilkinson (3)

Try: Jauzion
Conversion: Elissalde
Penalties: Elissalde (4), Michalak

After all the training and all the preparation, those England players remaining in the squad of thirty-six were itching to get a chance to play for their country in an international. Knowing that there would be one, final cull of six further players before the official squad of thirty was selected in the week following the second of three August warm-up Test matches, there was massive significance attached to being given the nod for the first game, against Wales at Twickenham. Head coach Brian Ashton had made it clear that he had only half a dozen names already as certainties for France 2007, so the players knew there was still much riding on the summer warm-up internationals, and especially the first two Tests. Getting first bite of the English cherry gave those players involved the chance to make an indelible case for the World Cup. Get it wrong, however, and the opportunity could prove to be your final stab at potential World Cup glory.

It was with much anticipation, therefore, from the world of rugby, and especially from within the England camp, that Ashton's twenty-two were announced for the Welsh game. It was, to say the least, full of surprises. In a new-look central midfield Andrew Farrell was given first crack at securing his place at inside centre while, outside him, Danny Hipkiss was awarded with a first cap. Farrell, the former rugby league legend who captained both Wigan and Great Britain to much success, had experienced a difficult two years since switching codes, through a whole spate of injuries, and an argument over which was his best position, back row or centre. Even in the recently finished June tour of South Africa, in which a depleted England squad were twice thrashed by a first-choice Springbok side, Farrell's ill health robbed him of a chance of some much-needed Test match practice, but now he had the opportunity to make his mark.

Leicester's Hipkiss would almost certainly have made his debut during that June tour of the Tigers had he not been playing in the Heineken Cup final, which meant that all Leicester, Wasps and Bath (who played in the European Challenge Cup final) players stayed back home in England. By common consent the outstanding centre of the 2006-07 Guinness Premiership season, Hipkiss now saw an opening to make a late charge for World Cup selection and he intended to make the most of it.

Elsewhere Mark Cueto, a destructive, high-scoring winger both for the Sale Sharks and England, was asked to play at full back, with Jason Robinson and David Strettle taking up their berths on the wings. Phil Vickery, named by Ashton as his World Cup captain at the start of the year, returned as captain, after first Robinson and then Jonny Wilkinson had led England in South Africa, while hooker Mark Regan's unlikely renaissance was confirmed by his selection to face Wales. The Bristol hooker had retired from international rugby under Andy Robinson, but had been on the phone to Ashton to announce he had performed a U-turn. Nick Easter started at No. 8, which meant former England captain Lawrence Dallaglio had to make do with a seat on the reserves' bench, while Martin Corry was employed as a blindside flanker.

Head coach Ashton explained why Corry, seen as a No. 8 or second row, would be wearing the number six jersey. 'I ask my players to be adaptable and flexible and I need to be the same,' he said. 'Having Martin in the back row dramatically increases our lineout options but that doesn't mean he will not be playing in the second row somewhere down the line.'

Perhaps the most interesting and heart-warming pick was in the second row, where Simon Shaw was given the chance to prove himself once again in an England jersey on the eve of a World Cup, this time alongside Steve Borthwick. For Shaw, now aged thirty-four, and considered by his club team-mates at Wasps to be their best player, year in, year out, the Rugby World Cup had proved to be something of a nemesis. Despite first gaining selection for the national squad thirteen years before, he had never played in a World Cup. In 1995 he missed out on travelling to South Africa with a ruptured knee. In 1999 he failed to make the final cut and, four years later, despite some storming performances in the warm-up games, he missed out again as Clive Woodward cited his play to be too similar to the England captain, Martin Johnson. In Woodward's seven years Shaw made just eleven starts.

'I did ask Clive why on occasions and he told me Johnno and I were too similar,' Shaw explained, as he viewed another chance to shine. 'If you could put two Martin Johnsons in your pack most teams would be happy, but he decided otherwise.'

The closest he came to playing in the World Cup was in Australia, in 2003, when Shaw was flown out to replace the injured Danny Grewcock, made it as far as the bench for the quarter-final against Wales, but never ventured on to the pitch. He collected a winner's medal after the final but it means very little to him. 'It was nice to be there but it would have meant so much more had I spent just five minutes on the pitch,' he admitted.

With World Cup winning lock Ben Kay in the squad, but not in the twenty-two for the Wales game, Shaw knew the competition for places remained high, and past experience had taught him that even his best may not be good enough. The 6ft 7in giant had played a pivotal role for England in their 43-9 win in Cardiff four years ago, just prior to the World Cup squad being selected by Woodward, but still he fell short.

'I was man of the match that day so it was a surprise that I was omitted,' Shaw mused. 'I don't think I could have done much more. Your confidence takes a knock every time you don't get selected but I never gave up on the hope of playing for England again. I believe in my own ability. Now it's just a question of whether the coaches do.'

It was good to see wing David Strettle back, as well, after his impressive start to his international career during the Six Nations. His progress had got seriously dented by a virus caught on the South African tour that hit him the hardest and resulted in the Harlequins player lying seriously ill in the intensive care unit of a Johannesburg hospital. 'I was struggling to breathe,' the twenty-four-year-old recalled. 'I was in a bad way and glad to get to hospital.' Fully recovered, and with weight regained, Strettle was excited to get another chance in an England jersey. 'It may be seen as a warm-up game but I will be as thrilled as when I ran out for my first international at Croke Park,' he admitted. 'Everyone wants a World Cup place and there's terrific competition within the squad.'

Another excited player, despite having done and seen it all in rugby league, was Farrell. Like Strettle, illness ruined his South Africa tour but now he had been made defensive captain by England defence coach Mike Ford and relished the responsibility. 'Some people see it as a trial game, but I suppose every match for your country is a trial because you want to play in the next one,' admitted Faz, as he is universally known. 'I'm obviously excited about playing again. We have to play well as a team otherwise the past few weeks will have been wasted.'

In typical fashion hooker Mark 'Ronnie' Regan, who recalled no-nonsense midweek evening encounters for Bristol at places such as Pontypridd and Bridgend, dispelled any myths that this would be a gentle afternoon's friendly game. 'I can't see it being a friendly at all,' he suggested, in his familiar Bristol burr. 'They smashed us at the Millennium Stadium a few months ago and now they're coming to the home of rugby. It's massive that we win. Massive for the team, the coaches and the country.'

While England chose a strong-looking twenty-two, Wales opted instead for a number of fringe players

'I can't see it being a friendly at all'

Mark Regan

27

who were clearly fighting to make up the extra numbers in the Welsh World Cup thirty. Although Gareth Thomas would lead the side, outside the experienced Tom Shanklin in the midfield, and Colin Charvis would start at No. 8, the rest of the starting XV were reserves, and most of the bench, too, save for James Hook, Gethin Jenkins and Alix Popham.

If the purpose was to see which Welsh players would play themselves into the World Cup squad, the outcome was to prove, instead, who should not be going to France. After two heavy defeats in South Africa, and a loss in Cardiff to a far stronger Wales XV in the final game of the Six Nations tournament, England got back to winning ways in some style. Nine tries, a record score, a record margin of victory over Wales and a record four tries by Nick Easter summed up a perfect afternoon's work-out for England as they romped to a 62-5 win over a very sorry looking Welsh outfit.

With a possibility that these two nations could meet again in the World Cup quarter-finals in France, depending on results in the pool stages, it was a good time for England to show their ruth-less side, and a bad time for Wales, even if it was a second- and third-choice squad, to ship a record points haul.

Just about the only thing that went wrong for England was the loss of Cueto to a groin injury during the warm-up. Matthew Tait came in at full back, and Toby Flood took up his fellow Newcastle Falcon's spot on the bench.

Despite this, the points flowed thick and fast in a first half in which Wales failed to threaten the English line once while the England pack grabbed their counterparts by the scruff of the neck and never let go. Their first try was well constructed after Shaun Perry's quick pass gave Wilkinson the chance to loft a high kick into the sun, which glared down on headquarters as temperatures reached 28 degrees Celsius. Lee Byrne was sacked by Robinson and, from the resulting ruck, Perry found a gap to dart through. The scrum half was brought down a couple of feet from the line but Easter picked up and drove over in the fourteenth minute.

The Harlequins No. 8 did it again seven minutes later after another Perry break and an almost identical pick up and drive over. On the half-hour Farrell, having returned from the blood bin with fifteen stitches and a bandage around his head, produced a meaningful break, fed Wilkinson and watched as the stand off's dancing feet gave Borthwick the chance to produce a bulldozing run. The Bath lock was brought down a metre from the line but rose to barge his way over.

It was more of the same after the break, despite the fact that captain Vickery failed to emerge after an ankle strain which he later played down. Matt Stevens replaced him, Corry took the captain's armband and, within four minutes, Easter had completed his hat-trick, once more crashing over from a metre out. Lawrence Dallaglio watched all this from the touchline, grinning ruefully and hoping that his chance would come.

It did, but not before Easter claimed a fourth try as he appeared to touch down in tandem with Perry on fifty minutes. It would be the forward's last act on a day that saw him become the first English No. 8 to score four tries in a match and only the third forward to do so, after Neil Back against Holland in 1998 and George Burton against Wales in 1881.

On came Dallaglio to a loud roar from the 66,000 crowd. Wales, ringing the changes, managed to get themselves on the scoreboard with a Dafydd James try in the corner but Dallaglio would have his say in the sixty-sixth minute, producing a classic No. 8 try by shepherding the ball at the base of the ruck, then picking up and forcing over. The World Cup winner's impact from the bench was in evidence again seven minutes from time when his clever pass gave man of the match Perry the chance to score a deserved try. There was still time for Robinson to score with a late chip and chase and for Tait to touch down Wilkinson's clever kick through to round off a thoroughly satisfying day for English rugby.

Nobody was getting too carried away with this. Wales, after all,

'I fancied some of the action, which is why I called for the scrum prior to my try'

Lawrence Dallaglio

had provided their worst display ever at Twickenham and, with the French coming to the same ground in seven days' time, England knew stiffer challenges lay ahead. But that night everyone had an understandable smile on their faces, not least Nick Easter, who really laid down a marker in his battle with Dallaglio to be the first choice No. 8.

'I could have told Lawrence that I'd softened them up for him to get one, but I didn't need to say anything,' Easter explained later, referring to the moment where Dallaglio took his place on the pitch. 'He knew exactly what to do and went out and did it.'

Dallaglio agreed. 'I watched Nick score four tries and it went through my mind that I'd better do something,' said the Wasps captain. 'I fancied some of the action, which is why I called for the scrum prior to my try. I wasn't bothered in the slightest that Nick did so well, just pleased to see England produce such a performance. I received a fantastic reception from the Twickenham crowd when I came on and, having seen Nick raise the bar high, it was my job to raise the bar higher.'

It was an entirely different England twenty-two named by head coach Brian Ashton to take on France the following week. Mike Catt, captain during the Six Nations for the win over France and defeat by Wales, was back at the helm, with Phil Vickery on the bench, allowing tight-head Stevens the chance to start. Ben Kay was in for Borthwick, while a back row of Dallaglio, Lewis Moody and James Haskell was a complete change from that which faced the Welsh. In the backs, Olly Barkley got his chance to stake a claim to the reserve spot as fly half behind Wilkinson, Jamie Noon lined up outside Catt, while Paul Sackey on the wing, and Nick

Abendanon at full back, also had their chance to bid for a World Cup place, with Sackey seemingly in a far stronger position than the South African-born youngster.

Barkley's selection, with Flood having played his part the week before, appeared to be the death-knell for Charlie Hodgson who, having missed the 2003 World Cup through injury, had been trying everything to recover in time from a right knee injury. Judging by this England twenty-two, time had just run out for the Sale Shark. 'Charlie has been very unlucky,' admitted Barkley. 'In terms of the intensity of the training it's been really hard for him to progress. I will miss Charlie. He's a really good friend and a fantastic player.'

Another World Cup dream appeared to be over, too, with the news that No. 8 Dan Ward-Smith had left the England camp and rejoined Bristol at their pre-season camp in France. The uncapped forward, one of the star players of the previous season, had, like Hodgson, made a valiant effort to recover from a fractured kneecap sustained the previous January but, yet again, it was deemed too much of a risk to take a player not quite recovered from a serious injury to the World Cup.

Far worse news was to strike England on the Wednesday before the France game when David Strettle collapsed in a heap during non-contact sprint training at England's base in Bath. It emerged that the fifth metatarsal bone in his left foot had snapped, the same kind of injury that had hit footballers such as David Beckham and Wayne Rooney in recent years. Strettle, although not playing at the weekend, was seen to be England's first choice right-wing but now it seemed his World Cup was over before it had even started. 'How the injury happened is a complete mystery because David was nowhere near anyone when it happened,' a bemused Ashton reported later. 'It was just a case of running with the ball and changing direction. It really doesn't look good at all.'

Two England players Strettle's injury would affect more than most were wingers Paul Sackey and Josh Lewsey. Both felt for the youngster, and also recognised what needed to be done. 'David's a very exciting player who's been playing really well,' said Sackey. 'To lose him would be a massive blow, but if that happens we've just got to get on with it. I shall be going out, though, as if David is fully fit and nothing has changed.'

Lewsey felt the same. 'What's happened to David is very regrettable and I'm gutted for him,' he responded. 'Not only is he a great lad who's had a fantastic season, but he also brings a winning mentality to the squad. He's always positive in everything he does and is full of confidence. Hopefully he will still have two or three World Cups in him. As for me, the last couple of years have been frustrating but now I'm raring to go.'

A scan the next day confirmed the worst. Strettle would not be able to play rugby again until after the World Cup was over. 'I felt that, step by step, I was getting closer to every player's dream and that's playing in the World Cup,' an understandably dejected Strettle explained. 'It's just such a massive disappointment. I was doing some open running. I took a side-step and just heard a crunch. I suspected something was broken and now I need to have screw inserted to repair the damage. It's very hard to take.'

In contrast Mike Catt, the great survivor, was back as captain and, at thirty-six years of age, insistent that he was as good as ever. 'I'm doing everything in training that the young boys are doing and I don't feel any slower than anyone,' said the man whose punt high into the stands at Sydney's Telstra Stadium denoted the end of the 2003 World Cup final. 'I've never felt better in my life. It's been a very different build-up to 2003. Then I went on the beer for five weeks in Spain before being called up at the last minute. After that I had an eight-week holiday in Australia with a bit of rugby thrown in. The volume of work we've done over the last six weeks has been

'You just put your head down and bosh on'

Mike Catt

immense. I've done every session, often four times a day. You just put your head down and bosh on. I'll be very disappointed if I'm not up to it, physically.'

One man who definitely ended the week disappointed was Lewis Moody. The Leicester flanker reported a slight tear in a calf muscle and Ashton, having already lost Strettle that week, had no hesitation in withdrawing Moody from the game against France. 'It was too big a risk,' Ashton explained. 'There was always the possibility that playing would make it worse to the point where he could be out for six weeks. We don't like to see anyone get injured so close to World Cup selection. Lewis had been looking forward to the opportunity of showing what he can do but it's not a long-term injury.' Joe Worsley therefore came into the side in the unusual position for him as open-side, with Steve Borthwick clambering on to the bench.

Everyone who was due to face the French understood the enormity of the occasion. It was a last chance to curry favour before the World Cup squad was announced. For Jamie Noon, who was cruelly cut from the final World Cup squad four years ago, knew exactly what he had to do. 'My destiny is in my own hands,' he admitted. 'Getting to the World Cup has been a goal of mine ever since I was a kid playing our own World Cup final in the back garden. In that respect my Newcastle team-mate Wilko has lived the dream and that's something I've always wanted to do.'

Noon would go on to enjoy a decent performance the following afternoon at Twickenham, but it was still back down to earth when England were taught a harsh lesson by a clinical France side who sucked in much of the pressure thrown at them to emerge as winners by 15-21. England may have led at half time, and they may have led deep into the second half, but they failed to cross over the French line while the man mountain that is Sebastian Chabal stormed up field late in the game to score the decisive try and hand France a major boost before they hosted the World Cup. Man of the match Chabal brought back unhappy memories of

Jonah Lomu as he crashed through a series of challenges, but England, who enjoyed massive territorial and positional advantage, had only themselves to blame for this ill-deserved defeat.

Olly Barkley began the day's proceedings with a smartly taken ninth-minute penalty to give England the lead. Knowing that a poor performance could yet result in World Cup omission, the Bath back converted the pressure kick well to ease his nerves and edge him closer to the back-up stand off position behind Jonny Wilkinson.

Three minutes later France took over the lead after a period of concerted pressure inside the England 22 resulted in a try on the wing for, of all people, Fabien Pelous. The French lock, equalling Philippe Sella's French caps record of 111, was lurking on the right wing when David Skrela's long, looping pass evaded Josh Lewsey. The former French captain had enough power to evade Lewsey's despairing tackle, a score confirmed by the television match official. Already it was clear that this would be no repeat of the previous week's demolition of Wales.

France, after all, were the Six Nations champions and World Cup hosts and, having named their squad for the tournament two months before, came to Twickenham with a starting XV not far off their strongest selection. In contrast, England had chosen a side designed to help head coach Ashton decide on his own final selection of the England World Cup squad, which was due to be named the following Tuesday. Any team without captain Vickery, Wilkinson and Robinson was a lesser England outfit, although Mike Catt, standing in as skipper, and Lawrence Dallaglio, starting an England Test for the first time in three years, would have begged to differ. Yet it was the visitors who increased their lead in the seventeenth minute when Skrela struck home a penalty after hooker Mark Regan was penalised for coming in at the side.

Back came England in spirited fashion, however. Barkley reduced the arrears with a penalty after Rémy Martin was caught offside, and then nudged England ahead after a trademark big hit from Noon on Clément Poitrenaud resulted in another penalty. Skrela regained the advantage following an altercation between French captain Rafael Ibanez and Regan, but Barkley and England had the last word before the break with a further penalty after Skrela failed to roll away.

After the interval Lee Mears came on for Regan and Andy Gomarsall for Shaun Perry, and the new scrum half increased England's lead in the fifty-fifth minute with a close-range drop goal. This signalled the introduction of the heavyweights from both sides, with Vickery and Martin Corry replacing Matt Stevens and Shaw, and Chabal, Yannick Nyanga and Frédéric Michalak swapping with Pelous, Serge Betsen and Damien Traille. Jean-Baptiste Elissalde had earlier come on for Pierre Mignoni, and it was the French scrum half who narrowed the English lead down to just one point again with a penalty on the hour.

England then had the chance to finish the job after making the most of a Michalak mis-kick. A smart move involving Nick Abendanon, Noon and Lewsey saw the ball reach Joe Worsley. With Paul Sackey outside him, all Worsley needed to do was pass out to the winger and it would have been game over. To be fair to the flanker, he caught Lewsey's pass low and way in front of him, making it nigh on impossible for him to see his fellow Wasps team-mate outside him. Instead he passed inside to a rampaging Phil Vickery who was halted a fingertip from the touchline by France's reserve hooker, Dimitri Szarzewski, who pulled off the tackle of the game. The chance went begging and within moments France shot up field and when Chabal collected 35 metres out, he stormed through Abendanon's challenge, brushed Lewsey off and crashed over in the corner. Elissalde converted and England's one-point lead had been transformed into a six-point deficit with just eight minutes remaining.

On came Wilkinson as a last throw of the dice and when Sackey went over in the corner the crowd erupted, but referee Alan Lewis had rightly blown ages earlier after Abendanon had knocked

'When you create the opportunities we did, you expect international players to finish them off'

Brian Ashton

on. It would prove to be England's last missed chance, and the game ended with a defeat on the last home occasion before the start of the World Cup.

'When you create the opportunities we did, you expect international players to finish them off,' was Brian Ashton's verdict afterwards. 'Maybe it was the excitement of getting into those positions but players at this level should be able to conquer that mental process. The camp is angry more than frustrated. They are just absolutely furious that they let the game get away. It's a hard lesson to learn but, thank God, we learn it now and not at the World Cup.'

Twenty-four hours later he would be sitting down with his fellow coaches to finalise the England World Cup squad of thirty and the collective verdict would be to go with experience. Indeed, the English squad playing in France would go down as the oldest set of players in the history of the tournament, with Mike Catt reaching 36 years of age in September, Lawrence Dallaglio and Mark Regan both 35, Perry Freshwater and Simon Shaw would both be 34 by the start of the tournament and Martin Corry would join them during the tournament. A host of others were also the wrong side of 30, which meant that, just as they were called back in 2003, England would once more be labelled 'Dad's Army'.

The squad pretty much picked itself except for one or two key areas. Jamie Noon's defensive strengths, so evident against France during the weekend just gone, got him ahead of Mike Tindall, whose broken leg the previous Easter made his inclusion unlikely, and the two youngsters, Nick Abendanon and Danny Cipriani. Prop Kevin Yates missed out to Freshwater, who would be filling the fourth prop's berth behind captain Vickery, Andrew Sheridan and Matt Stevens, while Mark Regan's amazing comeback from retirement meant that he joined George Chuter and Lee Mears as England's three hookers. Behind them Corry, who doubled up as both a lock and a back row forward, Ben Kay, Simon Shaw and Steve Borthwick would make up the second row department, with Dallaglio, Nick Easter, Joe Worsley, Lewis Moody and Tom Rees filling up the back row slots, making James Haskell the unlucky player to miss out.

In the backs, Peter Richards and Andy Gomarsall joined the seemingly first-choice scrum half, Shaun Perry, while Olly Barkley was number two fly half behind Jonny Wilkinson. Toby Flood was the unlucky youngster to miss the trip. The four centres were Mike Catt, Andy Farrell, Jamie Noon and Dan Hipkiss, who had done enough at the eleventh hour to receive Brian Ashton's vote of confidence, while the back three would be represented by Jason Robinson, Josh Lewsey, Mark Cueto, Paul Sackey and Matthew Tait. In all there were six remaining survivors from the 2003, World Cup-winning final XV – Vickery, Wilkinson, Robinson, Dallaglio, Lewsey and Kay, and another seven from the squad of thirty.

The next day the head coach announced the twenty-two to face France in the warm-up re-match in Marseille. In an ideal world, England's strongest XV would be known but Ashton admitted the night-time encounter in Provence would be the stage for a series of final selection eliminators, and none more so than the battle for the No. 8 spot between Easter and Dallaglio, with the former starting.

'Rather than ride around in an armchair like he did against Wales, Nick gets the opportunity now in a match where it's possible he will spend at least half the game on the back foot,' Ashton explained. 'We'll see how he copes with that. Nick has now got to put a marker down, saying: "Look, I can handle this game in Marseille. I can show I am good enough to be the top No. 8."

Lawrence handled the game last week, played for eighty minutes and is ready to play again this week. He'll get some game time on Saturday.'

Indeed, Ashton was at pains to praise the former England captain, especially in light of recent suggestions made by Will Carling, the 1991 England World Cup captain, that the Wasps man was a 'divisive influence'.

'Lawrence has been the complete opposite,' Ashton insisted. 'His presence has made the squad stronger. I see him as both a starter and an impact player off the bench. It would be wrong to say Nick is above Lawrence in the pecking order but it's good to have that competition there right to the end of the warm-up games. I said I wanted to name my strongest team for this match and, had we played France twice over the last two Saturdays, I probably would have been able to do so, but it's not possible given the massive difference in the games against Wales and France in terms of intensity and the strength of the opposition. Given the nature of the Welsh game – something which we couldn't control – it would be really unfair to judge a group of thirty players on a game like that and a very different game last Saturday. We are under no illusions that if we continue to play like we have, we might get somewhere in the World Cup but we won't get to where we ultimately want to be. With stats like the sixty per cent possession and sixty per cent territory we had last Saturday you've got to be winning. We want to go to France and redress the balance by beating them in their own backyard.'

> 'We want to go to France and redress the balance by beating them in their own backyard'
>
> *Brian Ashton*

In total, twelve new players came in from the side that lost at home to France. Only Josh Lewsey on the wing, Shaun Perry at scrum half and Simon Shaw at lock remained. Mark Cueto, Dan Hipkiss, Andy Farrell,

Jason Robinson, Jonny Wilkinson, Perry Freshwater, George Chuter, Phil Vickery, Steve Borthwick, Martin Corry, Tom Rees and Easter all came in. Freshwater got his chance to prove himself thanks to an insect which, having bitten Andrew Sheridan's right leg, did enough damage to send the big prop to a hospital in Bath where the Sale Shark was placed on a course of antibiotics.

Elsewhere other mini trials would also be taking place, notably in the midfield. 'Some are playing in positions where others last week put down big markers, like Jamie Noon,' Ashton continued. 'It's a big game for Dan Hipkiss and a big game, too, for Andy Farrell and George Chuter. Ben Kay was outstanding last week and now Steve Borthwick's got to show he can do the same. So it's another trial. There's no point trying to hide it.'

The battle for the first-choice No. 8 berth had both participants talking. Dallaglio was miffed by Carling's suggestions. 'I am certainly not divisive,' he insisted. 'Otherwise I wouldn't be here. I've been brought back because I'd like to think one of the things I can do is bring a team together rather than split it apart.' He was equally positive about his role in the battle with Easter. 'My initial role is a supporting one, not just for Nick but for everyone in the team,' he added. 'If you feel you have something positive to contribute to the game then you say so. It's a twenty-two-man game these days and not a case of dog eat dog. We're a team and it's essential we operate as one. You give the team your full support, whether you like it or not. When the boot is on the other foot and it's your turn, you expect the same.'

Easter, meanwhile, found himself in pole position in the battle. For a man who had arrived at this juncture via Old Alleynians, Ilkeston, Rosslyn Park, Villagers of Cape Town, Orrell, Rotherham and Harlequins, it was quite an achievement to be keeping Dallaglio out. 'I have a lot more to show,' he promised. 'It's great to have a world-class player like Lawrence pushing me along. The more time I occupy the No. 8 shirt, the less time there is for somebody else.'

Another 2003 hero, Jonny Wilkinson, was in a positive mood and far from downbeat about England's prospects. 'I don't think I have ever been as in control or better prepared, physically, as I am right now,' said the man who had missed so much rugby in between World Cups through injury. 'I am ready to go.'

He also backed the squad of England players he would be travelling to France with. 'You look around and see guys who are not fazed by what they are about to face,' Wilkinson continued. 'You see players who have been through the toughest challenges over and over again, whether it be World Cups, Grand Slams, Lions tours or European Cups. They bring presence and stability. For those who do not have as much experience, they bring assurance. These guys are all in great physical condition. Most of them will say they are better than they've ever been. All being well, there are a good few years ahead of me as well.'

Mark Cueto felt the same although, after a groin injury sustained in warm-up just before the start of the Twickenham Test against Wales, he would settle for just surviving the next game, first, and a game in which he would be asked to fill the troubled spot of full back.

'I stepped off my right foot and as I planted my left I felt a twang in my groin,' explained the Cumbrian, re-living that warm-up injury. 'Luckily, I was only going at fifty per cent, otherwise it might have caused more damage. I've been doing the same pre-match routine for seven years and never had any trouble. Fortunately, it was nothing more than a niggle but I might take another couple of minutes being a bit more cautious over my warm-up in future.'

As a winger Cueto had more than proved his worth, scoring 13 tries in just 18 Tests, but now he was asked to wear the full back's jersey having made the switch at Sale. 'Things were going well for me at Sale and England on the wing and I didn't want to jeopardise a possible place at the World Cup by trying to mix and match positions,' he said. 'My getting injured and other wings coming through made the switch happen probably six months sooner than intended. We talk about the back three as a unit. The positions are interchangeable so, as a wing, you can spend almost as much time covering at full back. That's made the switch easier for me.'

There was nothing easy about Saturday night, though. Very little that had been hoped for actually happened in Marseille. England succumbed to a French team that, in truth, played below their best and missed so many kicking and try-scoring opportunities that the visitors were lucky not to concede 40 points. The facts backed this up, and made for not good reading from an English viewpoint. England failed to score a try for the second Test in as many weeks against France, and they failed to break the gain line once. In an error-strewn display, with 14 handling and 24 kicking mistakes, England gave a French team dominant in possession and territory every opportunity to win. Les Bleus did not need a second invitation.

Sporting their new red away kit for the first time, England ran determinedly out on to the pitch to be met by a cacophony of jeers by the large, partisan home support. This re-match between two old adversaries was brimming with passion and tempo at the Stade Vélodrome, a venue so notorious for visiting teams that only Argentina had ever won there. Inside the first twenty minutes, Farrell was involved in a fracas with both Damien Traille and Imanol Harinordoquy, Martin Corry and Fabien Pelous had swapped punches, and there were various other minor spats, forcing referee Alain Rolland to conduct a long lecture to the two captains, Wasps team-mates Phil Vickery and Raphaël Ibanez.

In between all this, England at first matched the French. Jonny Wilkinson kicked England into a fourteenth-minute lead with a penalty, which they held for just two minutes before Jean-Baptiste Elissalde equalised. Boasting a back line which included Yannick

Jauzion and Christophe Dominici, the World Cup hosts began to probe away at the English defence. Elissalde kicked two further penalties in the thirty-fourth and thirty-eighth minutes. With seconds remaining of the first half England were dealt a double blow. Simon Shaw was sent to the sin bin for a high tackle on Traille and Vickery was carried off on a stretcher, having been knocked unconscious when caught up in the collision involving Shaw and Traille. Elissalde kicked the penalty given for Shaw's offence and England, minus their captain, returned to the half-time dressing room nine points adrift.

Matt Stevens replaced Vickery after the break and Wilkinson reduced the arrears with a forty-first-minute penalty, but back came France with a vengeance. Yannick Nyanga should have passed but chose instead to go for the English tryline, only to see Wilkinson knock the ball out of his hand as he dived over, a decision confirmed by the TV match official. Moments later Jauzion crashed through Shaun Perry and Andy Farrell to score close enough to the posts to make Elissalde's fiftieth-minute conversion a formality. France's one-man advantage had proved crucial.

Shaw returned and Wilkinson kicked his third penalty to hand his men hope. Paul Sackey and Joe Worsley came on for Josh Lewsey and Tom Rees, then Lawrence Dallaglio replaced Nick Easter, meaning that England had run out of forward replacements by the time Martin Corry was forced off with what looked like a worrying knee injury. When Steve Borthwick trampled all over Imanol Harinordoquy, the resulting penalty saw Michalak ease France into an unassailable, 13-point lead.

Just three weeks before the start of the World Cup and England's first pool game against the USA, this was a dispiriting setback. The plan was to win, or at least pose the French some searching questions. Instead, having lost two out of three of their World Cup warm-up games – and the first choice Wales XV's defeat of Argentina that same weekend put their reserves who took on England into perspective – England faced a barrage of criticism

'We can play a lot better than that and we'll need to'

Mike Catt

and were given little hope, on this evidence, of getting even close to defending successfully their world title.

'We're going to be heavily criticised and written off all the more,' predicted Dallaglio afterwards. 'That will make us stronger as a group. There are no safety nets now, no more second chances. From now on it's for real. People will be a bit downbeat but we need to stick together and raise our game by at least twenty per cent.'

Mike Catt was another senior figure in the squad who spoke frankly about the situation England found themselves in. 'I thought we'd be further ahead than we are,' said the South African-born Catt. 'The World Cup is going to be a massive ask for us now.'

Catt had played no part in the game but instead sat in the stands and watched France dismantle his team-mates. 'We can play a lot better than that and we'll need to if we stand any chance of venturing far at the World Cup,' he added. 'Some of the boys are not too happy with the criticism we've had from the media and from the English rugby supporters, but the reality is we've done nothing to shout about. We need to face up to a few home truths.'

What upset Catt most about the Marseille defeat was the fact that he believed before the game that England would win, a view based on what he had seen the previous week at Twickenham. 'I honestly felt we would beat the French because we should have done at Twickenham,' he said. 'I still don't quite know how we managed to lose the week before. It was just down to poor execution but I felt we'd got that right during the week and more composure was all that was needed. Instead we played very differently. We were too one-dimensional. Teams can defend very easily against us at the moment.'

Indeed they could. And this was England's last chance before the World Cup began for real. Four years previously, they had travelled down to Australia having already won there, and in New Zealand, a few months before. In the 2003 warm-up games they had scored handsome wins in Cardiff and at home against the French, and then a narrow defeat in Marseille when fielding a second XV, all of which had reinforced England's belief that they could become world champions.

Four years on and nobody inside the England camp could persuade themselves that everything had gone well in the build-up to the tournament. It had not, and they would be travelling to France more with hope and prayer rather than conviction. No wonder few gave them any chance at all to make an impact at the World Cup, which makes England's ultimate story that much more outrageous.

Chapter 2: Pool Game
England v USA

Saturday 8 September at the Stade Félix Bollaert, Lens *Attendance* 35,000

ENGLAND 28		USA 10
Cueto	15	Wyles
Lewsey	14	Sika
Noon	13	Emerick
Catt	12	Esikia
Robinson	11	Ngwenya
Barkley	10	Hercus (Captain)
Perry	9	Erskine
Sheridan	1	MacDonald
Regan	2	Lentz
(Captain) Vickery	3	Osentowski
Shaw	4	Parker
Kay	5	Mangan
Worsley	6	Stanfill
Rees	7	Clever
Dallaglio	8	Bloomfield

Replacements

Richards (for Perry) 60 mins
Chuter (for Regan) 63 mins
Farrell (for Catt) 63 mins
Stevens (for Vickery) 63 mins
Corry (for Shaw) 63 mins
Tait (for Robinson) 67 mins
Moody (for Worsley) 69 mins

Malifa (for Sika) 52 mins
Burdette (for Lentz) 53 mins
Basauri (for Bloomfield) 56 mins
Moeakiola (for MacDonald) 60 mins
Mexted (for Mangan) 69 mins

Referee   J.Kaplan (South Africa)

England	USA
Barkley (penalty) 7 mins	Hercus (penalty) 9 mins
Barkley (penalty) 22 mins	Moeakiola (try) 74 mins
Barkley (penalty) 31 mins	Hercus (conversion) 76 mins
Robinson (try) 35 mins	
Barkley (try) 40 mins	
Barkley (conversion) 40 mins	
Rees (try) 49 mins	
Barkley (conversion) 50 mins	

Match statistics

England		USA
3	Tries	1
2	Conversions	1
(3) 3	Penalties (taken)	1 (1)
0	Drop goals	0
9	Scrums won	12
0	Scrums lost	2
12	Lineouts won	13
3	Lineouts lost	3
3	Turnovers won	3
71	Tackles made	76
9	Tackles lost	20
4	Line breaks	1
54%	Possession	46%
62%	Territory	38%
10	Errors	9
26	Possession kicked	27
8	Penalties conceded	9
5'46"	Time in oppo 22	3'35"
1	Yellow cards	2
0	Red cards	0

England v USA Record

Overall	Played 5	England won 5
World Cup	Played 3	England won 3

Phil Vickery is your good, old-fashioned type of rugby player. He tells it how it is. There are no fancy sound-bites, no brash statements. His character is hewn from his down-to-earth upbringing on a Cornish farm. He was, as England head coach Brian Ashton would point out repeatedly, exactly his kind of captain. Like Martin Johnson before him, players would follow Vickery because he set an example by deeds more than by words. Sitting at home the day before England departed for French shores, the thirty-one-year-old Wasps prop spoke with brutal honesty about the position his England team found themselves in. 'There's no question, it's going to be really difficult to win the World Cup again,' he admitted. 'There's no hiding away from the fact. It's been tough being an England player ever since the last World Cup, both on and off the field. There's not been a single player in the squad who's not given his all, but it's not been enough, and we know we have to find something more.'

Vickery normally hid his emotions well but it was quite evident he did not enjoy captaining a losing national side. 'I take it personally,' he confirmed. 'And I ask myself questions every day about my own performance, both as a player and as a captain. It's during these times that I remind myself of a few facts: that I must be bloody good at what I do, I'm here for a reason and that somebody clearly backs me.'

By his own admission he was big enough, old enough and ugly enough to take any personal flak but, like any good leader, he was keen to protect his troops. 'When we got booed off after losing to Argentina I remember looking at some of our young newcomers in the team,' he recalled. 'It didn't

'I take it personally'

Phil Vickery

bother me and, yes, we were disappointing that day, but I looked at the bewilderment in their eyes and I felt for them. We're going to need all the support we can get in France and it would be nice to see everyone who supports England get behind the team.'

It might have been easier for Vickery if he had not accepted the captaincy role when Brian Ashton contacted him the previous January, especially if his standing as a crucial member of the World Cup-winning team was going to take a mauling over the next few weeks. Yet, to suggest he should have opted out was to insult a principled man. 'I play rugby because I love it,' he explained. 'Playing the other week in Marseille, even though we were poor in the second half, is what playing Test match rugby is all about. The atmosphere was unbelievable and it will be experiences like that you'll remember. If you're going to take the plaudits you have to accept the crap as well. I'm more than happy to be part of a building process with England. If this World Cup has come too soon, then so be it. If England miss out this time, but go on to be 2011 world champions, then no one will be happier than me. But if you don't want to experience setbacks, just because you've tasted success, that makes you a sad person.

'People have short memories, in any case. I was part of that England team that shipped seventy-six points to Australia in 1998. Even when we became world class we kept losing those Grand Slam-deciding Tests. We've been where we are now before and there's no quick fix.'

So was there any hope for England? Purely on form it appeared not, but Vickery made a case worth considering. 'I've experienced both sides of the coin in the World Cup,' he pointed out. 'In 1999 we lost to South Africa in the quarter-finals when one bloke scored five drop goals. I mean, where did that come from? We couldn't do anything about it. Four years later we may have been favourites, but I never thought we were definitely going to win it. We turned it round very late against Samoa, and we probably wouldn't have beaten Wales in the quarter-finals had Mike Catt not come on in the second half. We failed to score a try in the semi-finals and we all know how close it was in the final. So anything can happen. I hope I'll return home with another World Cup winner's medal but, failing that, at least we've shown the world what we're really capable of.'

Another man to speak with honesty was that quarter-final hero, Catt, who was about to embark on his fourth World Cup adventure. It began back in 1995 when England, led by Will Carling, beat Australia in a dramatic quarter-final, won by a last-gasp drop goal from Rob Andrew, only to lose heavily in the semi-final against a rampant New Zealand epitomised by a young and huge Tongan-born winger called Jonah Lomu who, that day, scored four tries, including one which saw him use Catt as a doormat. 'I can laugh about being trampled on by Lomu now,' Catt insisted. 'I mean, I was thirteen stone and he weighed a ton. My only regret is that he stumbled, which is why he ended up walking all over me. If he hadn't, I'm sure he would have sprinted round me instead.' Four years on and it was a freakish display from Jannie De Beer that did for England. 'I was on the bench but came on with Jonny Wilkinson with not long left to try to turn it around,' he recalled. 'The thing about De Beer that day is that there was nothing we could do to stop him. He was taking his drop goals from too far out for us to close him down. It was incredible to see them all go over, from all angles and from so far out.'

The memories from the next World Cup, in 2003, were very different, however, especially for Catt who had spent much of the previous season injured and slipped into Clive Woodward's squad only at the eleventh hour. It was his half-time introduction that turned a quarter-final deficit against Wales into victory and, even though he started against France in the semi-final, it was Catt's call that Mike Tindall should take his shirt for the final. 'I hadn't played for the best part of a year and I felt it during that semi-final,' he admitted. 'I'm very proud of the impact I made in the quarter-final, but Clive was right to start with Tindall and have me come on later in the game, and I told him so.' As for the final, Catt's memories were of joy and relief. 'I'm so glad I managed to kick that ball out of touch. Even then there were a few seconds left and I was worried Australia might be able to launch one last attack, but by the time we all made our way down the pitch the game was over.'

Had time run out for the England World Cup team of 2007, though? 'You have to be realistic,' he answered. 'New Zealand have been favourites for a long time and South Africa had a good Super 14 and Tri-Nations. France, as hosts, will be a big threat, Australia are always there or thereabouts and nobody should discount Ireland. So it's not going to be easy for us, especially if we carry on performing like we have. But I look around the team and I see so many world-class players. Our deficiencies may seem big but, in truth, they can easily be corrected. We're underdogs, and we have nothing to scream and shout about right now, but it's all about getting it right over the next seven weeks, not the past few months. We know exactly what we need to do. What we don't know is whether we can do it, but no one is happy in the England dressing-room about the way it's gone, and everybody wants to do something about it, starting from now.'

His head coach, Brian Ashton, admitted to being both excited and unsure of how the next few weeks would pan out. 'We're a squad that's only been together seven weeks, that's played three games with different personnel, and that's still evolving,' he admitted. 'There is an unknown factor but there's also the exciting mix of being world champions and underdogs at the same time.' Indeed, so lowly fancied were England to become the first nation ever to retain the World Cup that you could get odds of 33–1 against such a feat actually happening. 'We'll give it our best shot,' Ashton promised. 'That goes without saying, but this team has a lot more to offer than we have seen so far. There is no minimum ambition for a World Cup. You just have to get out there and win it. A lot of people have forgotten that we are still world champi-

'I think England will certainly get to the semi-finals'

Andy Robinson

ons. No team has ever successfully defended a rugby world title before and I see it as a fantastic opportunity for a team which has been written off all over the world. The players will use it as a motivation and make sure they come up with something a bit different when it matters most. We haven't shown it yet, and maybe that's been deliberate, but I'm confident we're more than capable of surprising people. This is the biggest challenge in my rugby career, by some distance. I have gone for players with big-game experience, players who have been through tough situations before with the mentality to cope with whatever is thrown at them.'

His predecessor, despite England's continuing indifferent results, gave Ashton's men a vote of confidence as they left for France to settle in to the team hotel, the Trianon Palace, in Versailles. 'I think England will certainly get to the semi-finals,' said Andy Robinson. 'If they do, they have the one-off players to get to the final.'

Certainly nothing was being left to chance. Rob Andrew, the RFU's elite director of rugby, revealed how England had strengthened their medical team in readiness for some potentially bruising encounters in the pool stages alone: against South Africa, and then the occasionally brutal Polynesians from Samoa then Tonga. 'We're looking at taking an additional masseur because there are probably no more physical teams anywhere in the world than the three in our pool,' he explained. 'When you could have the best part of your thirty players needing treatment for bumps and bruises, then you have to plan accordingly.

'There will be some very big sides at this tournament. When we get our biggest pack on to the field we will be as big as anyone. If you don't have that platform you have no chance on the world stage. That is what Brian Ashton and the coaches have been working really hard on over the last few weeks. We can see the impact they have had physically, but there are clearly some finishing and creation issues which the players will have to work on in the next three weeks. Our record since the last World Cup has been very poor all round, particularly away from home. There are lots of different reasons for that and I'd rather look forward than back. The coaches have had seven weeks to lay the foundations and select their squad but that has to be put into context of how little time they have had to do it all. The England players are a very determined group. They have worked incredibly hard over the last seven weeks, so hard that I would be surprised if any other squad anywhere in the world has worked any harder. I'm very confident they will give a very good account of themselves.'

They left for Paris from Heathrow on 3 September courtesy of British Airways, who renamed the 747 Jumbo 'Hope and Glory' in their honour. Simon Shaw was already in the wars, however, having contracted a facial skin infection requiring a shot of antibiotics even to travel. One of his team-mates in the second row, Ben Kay, shed a little light on where the team stood. 'We've tried very hard to recreate the pressure of the match situation in training,' he explained. 'Training sessions are shorter and undoubtedly more intense and more physical than matches. We all know the guys in the squad are good enough. The key now is to get some cohesion and playing together.'

On the Tuesday, the day after arriving in France, Ashton named his first squad of twenty-two men to play in the Rugby World Cup, and there was one significant omission. Jonny Wilkinson, the man who had come through twelve injuries since the 2003 final against Australia, seven of them serious, managed to twist his right ankle during training, was stretchered off the pitch and had been ruled out of England's opening game. In executing a defence drill, Steve Borthwick went to cover Phil Vickery, and Wilkinson, jumping out of the way, twisted his ankle in landing awkwardly. There was a real concern that the injury might also keep him out of the second pool game against South Africa some six days later. Losing Wilkinson for the USA match was one thing, playing without him against the rampant Springboks was quite another.

'Two people came in simulating a ruck and as they went to ground, Jonny, as one of the defenders, jumped out of the way and twisted his ankle with nobody near him,' explained Mike Ford, the defence coach. 'The initial pain was very severe but within a couple of minutes it had settled down. It's possible he could have done enough damage to put him out for more than one game. Should Jonny not be available against South Africa then we've just got to get on with it. Hopefully, it will be nothing serious. But we're not going to be negative any more. We talked about that even before today's training. We're getting pretty cheesed off that there may be excuses for us not to do well in the World Cup. It's time to stop using them.'

In terms of his other injuries experienced since 2003, this was not too bad. Wilkinson's medical list in the previous four years had made painful reading: a fractured right shoulder in December 2003 that kept him out for three weeks; an operation on his neck and shoulder in February 2004 that ruled him out for seven months; a haematoma to the upper right arm in October 2004 lost him another six weeks; medial ligament damage to his left knee in January 2005 cost him a further two months; an injury to his left knee in March of that year resulted in a month's lay-off; injuries to both his right arm and shoulder were followed by his appendix being removed in the summer of 2005; a groin strain and subsequent hernia operation then lost him two more months in November 2005; after that he suffered a torn adductor muscle in January 2006 that saw him out of the game for another three months. Medial ligament damage to the right knee resulted in another four-week lay-off that September, and a lacerated kidney two months later lost him six more weeks; finally, a pulled hamstring in February 2007 removed him for six weeks and the last three Six Nations matches. It is a quite incredible list of setbacks which said a great deal about the man's refusal to pack it in. In this light, a twisted ankle was just about the least serious injury of them all, but the timing could not have been worse. 'It was just one of those unfortunate things that happen every so often, but I spoke to him very briefly and he was as philosophical as ever,' Ashton added.

The England team was announced to the players at 9.45 in the morning. Training began forty-five minutes later and by 11.00 a.m. Olly Barkley, who had been named on the bench, suddenly found himself in for Wilkinson, one left-footed kicker replacing another. 'It was quite clear when it happened that Jonny was not able to continue training,' Barkley said. 'I looked round and saw him in a fair bit of pain.'

They may have been without Wilkinson for Saturday's opener against the USA, but England would still be featuring plenty of experience, with thirty-five-year-old Lawrence Dallaglio winning his personal battle with Nick Easter to take up the No. 8 berth in the starting XV (Easter failed to make the twenty-two). Mike Catt, who would be thirty-six the following week, was preferred to Andy Farrell at inside centre, with the former rugby league star named as one of the seven reserves only after Barkley was promoted into the starting XV following Wilkinson's mishap.

It would make England's kicking department look decidedly threadbare. With Toby Flood not surviving the final cutback the previous month for the World Cup squad, and Shane Geraghty dismissed prior to that, Farrell suddenly found himself next in line after Barkley and, while he had kicked over a thousand goals in rugby league, his union tally stood at one penalty and one conversion against Leicester for Saracens on New Year's Day, and one conversion at Worcester in April.

Hopefully, with Barkley starting, Farrell's kicking would not be required. The Bath back had acquitted himself well when he last

'You can't prepare yourself for someone falling down in training'

Olly Barkley

started for England in the home defeat to France in the warm-up international, and he was more than ready to seize his chance now.

'You can't prepare yourself for someone falling down in training,' the twenty-five-year-old Barkley said. 'It's not an ideal way to be starting, but it's an opportunity I have to make sure I take. The game is too important for me to dare look beyond it to the next one. Fingers crossed, Jonny will soon be fit. There is a bit more pressure because Jonny has created such an impression. Anyone following in the number ten position is always going to be compared to him. I'm not downhearted about that. I see it as a positive, a challenge to show that he has not raised the bar too high for me to reach. Goal-kicking is a pretty lonely job because it demands so much of your time on the training field. You end up getting back when everyone else has eaten their lunch. Usually, it's just me and Jonny out there when the rest have all gone. I'm not one for practising for as long as he does. I find I get stale after ninety minutes whereas Jonny goes for two or even two and a half hours. It certainly works for him. Watching Jonny and studying his technique is a huge boost and he's helped me massively, especially with my punting. As for the USA, I have to look on this as just another rugby match, rather than a game in the World Cup.'

Elsewhere Mark Cueto would start as full back, with Jason Robinson and Josh Lewsey on the wings, the latter winning his fiftieth cap. 'There was a time when I thought I wouldn't even make ten caps,' Lewsey reflected on hearing he was on the verge of completing his half century. Jamie Noon got the vote over Matthew Tait and Dan Hipkiss at outside centre while, in the back row, Dallaglio was joined by Tom Rees at open-side, and Joe Worsley beat Martin Corry to the blind-side position.

Corry, in fairness, had completed only one team run since twisting his left knee against France in Marseille eighteen days previously, so he had done well to regain enough fitness even to make the bench.

Ben Kay and Simon Shaw would make up the second row, while Andrew Sheridan and captain Vickery, as expected, would stand either side of hooker Mark Regan in the front row. With the likes of Corry, Farrell, Tait and Lewis Moody all on the bench, there was plenty of potential impact, too. The reserves were given cause for hope by their head coach who, having previously said that the team for the USA would be pretty much the team to face South Africa, was sounding less sure of himself. 'We have picked the best combination for this particular match,' remarked Ashton. 'We will then assess what is required for the following week.'

One day and one scan later, Wilkinson was making positive noises about his possible availability for the South Africa clash. Although the scan revealed a ligament sprain, the stand off was hopeful. 'While I am loath to be held to any sort of date, I am looking at the South Africa match as a game that I am hoping and still determined to play in,' he said.

With or without him, England's players were adamant they would be more than able to cope. 'We've got thirty players all as good as each other,' insisted Mark Regan, who was clearly enjoying his life back in international rugby. It was a view shared by scrum half Shaun Perry. 'Jonny is a legend and you can't take that away,' said Regan's Bristol team-mate. 'He does bring a bit of presence about him when he's playing, but we've got that in other players in the squad, too.'

Perspective was introduced to the reality of England's final few days preparing for the start of the World Cup by a sombre visit on the Thursday to the war memorial in Thiepval, near Lens, which bears the names of 72,000 soldiers, including many former English rugby international players, missing from the Battle of the Somme. Brian Ashton and Phil Vickery laid a poppy wreath at the

A dejected Martin Corry leads off the England side after their hugely disappointing defeat to Argentina in November 2006 – it was the Pumas' first victory at Twickenham. (PA)

(above) Brian Ashton was appointed head coach in December 2006 and had nine months to turn round England's stuttering form. One of his first acts was to appoint Phil Vickery (right) as England captain for the World Cup. (Getty Images)

ENGLAND
RUGBY

As part of England's World Cup warm-up, they went to Vilamoura in Portugal to prepare. After Simon Shaw's hard work building up his strength and stamina, he was joined by his team-mates in an ice bath. (Getty Images)

Nick Easter scores one of his record four tries against Wales on 4 August to put down his marker for the No. 8 role in England's World Cup team. But Lawrence Dallaglio was going to push him every step of the way, as he shows just how much scoring a try means to him. (Action Images)

After the 62-5 mauling of Wales, England's World Cup hopes were brought down to earth when Sébastien Chabal scored a late winning try. (PA)

Andy Farrell confronts Damien Traille during England's mistake-strewn final warm-up game in Marseille. (Getty Images)

The day before flying out to France, Mike Catt and the rest of the squad help out young fans at the Scrum in the Park. (Corbis)

The England team pose on the steps of 'Hope and Glory', the plane that flew them to France on 3 September. (Getty Images)

Simon Shaw poses outside the Trianon Palace Hotel in Versailles, England's World Cup base. (Reuters/Corbis/Eddie Keogh)

Not again! Jonny Wilkinson studies his injured right ankle on the first day of training in France. He was to miss the first two matches of the tournament. (Getty Images)

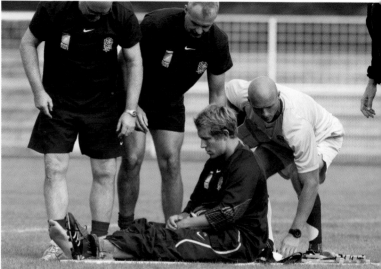

Olly Barkley evades the tackle of Alec Parker to score his try at the end of the first half to send England in with a comfortable 21-3 lead over the USA. (Colorsport)

Tom Rees powers over the line to claim England's third try against the USA – but alarmingly England could not add to their score in the last half-hour. (Getty Images)

Phil Vickery trips Paul Emerick and was subsequently banned for two matches when he was cited after the game. (Getty Images)

In England's vital pool match against South Africa, only Jason Robinson seemed to have any answers, being resolute under the high ball and inspired in attack, but even he had to be helped from the field when injury struck. (Action Images/PA)

Dejected England players reflect on their record World Cup defeat after losing 36-0 to South Africa. (Getty Images)

foot of the memorial as the whole of the England squad looked on, deep in thought and quite clearly taken aback by an occasion Ashton would later describe as 'frightening and inspiring'. His grandfather, the head coach revealed, had also fought at the Somme and was one of the lucky ones to return home. 'It gives us all a sense of perspective,' he added. Ashton discovered four name-sakes who were Lancashire Fusiliers and were possible distant relatives. Josh Lewsey found two Lewseys among the names and believed he was related to them.

Meanwhile, as part of their preparations, the American team had visited the American Second World War cemetery and memorial at Omaha Beach in Normandy on the previous Monday. They would not be expecting any favours from England come Saturday evening. Only four members of the squad were profes-sionals. Centre Paul Emerick played in Wales for Newport; prop Mike MacDonald at Leeds; lock Luke Gross at Doncaster; and right wing Salesi Sika for Beziers in France. Their captain, Mike Hercus, used to play at stand off for Sale.

There was a time when American rugby was on top of the world. In 1920 they won the Olympic gold medal in Antwerp employing American footballers. They repeated the feat, beating France in Paris four years later using tactics so physical that the crowd rioted in disgust and 500 gendarmes were required to remove the American players safely from the pitch. The International Olympic Association reacted by kicking the sport out of its Games and this has remained the case, despite rugby's many efforts to be reinstated, ever since, thus making America the longest-serving reigning Olympic champions. In more recent times, there has been little success for the Eagles. In thirteen pre-vious matches spread over four World Cup tournaments they have managed just two wins, and both of those were against Japan. Preparations for the 2007 tournament had not gone too well, either. After being thrashed by Canada and then conceding 50 points to an English third-string team in the Churchill Cup while

'Rugby's not really on the radar in the States'

Nigel Melville

those not playing in European Cup finals were out on tour in South Africa, the USA lost their final warm-up game in Chicago to Munster's reserves.

But at least they did have Nigel Melville on board. Melville, the former England captain and former Wasps and Gloucester coach, was American rugby's chief executive. 'Rugby's not really on the radar in the States,' Melville admitted. 'We're not daft enough to pretend there isn't a gap between us and England, but the players' aim is to upset the applecart. They know they have to play better than they have ever played before. As amateurs, they have put their lives on hold to be here, in many cases giving up their jobs. These guys have made great sacrifices.'

Ironically, their captain, former Sale Shark Mike Hercus, played against Jonny Wilkinson eleven years previously in a schoolboy international. Being robbed of the chance of a re-match due to Wilkinson's injury hardly appeared to make his task much easier. 'I'm more concerned about the England pack than I would have been about Jonny,' was his take on the news that the English first choice stand off was out. 'The pack helps him achieve what he does so well.'

At last the waiting was over. Phil Vickery, for one, could not wait to get it on. 'The time for talking is over,' he declared. 'Now it's time for action. Nobody gives us much of a chance, which is great because we're going to show some people what we're capable of. Everyone is itching to get started. We want to get out there and do what we love, which is to win games. We have to deliver a performance to be proud of because the pressure is on. We all know South Africa is looming large on the horizon next week.'

The expectations were high for their first World Cup game in Lens. Having not scored a try in their last two internationals,

'The time for talking is over. Now it's time for action'

Phil Vickery

against France in the warm-up games in August, England were expected to cross the American whitewash on numerous occasions, but Ashton was keen to keep a lid on predictions. 'Once you start talking about the number of points you are going to score, you are in very dangerous territory,' he explained. 'The important thing is to get the key to the performance right and then the result will follow. We can cause all sorts of problems for all sorts of teams in the next few weeks. I have every confidence in the team's ability to rise to the occasion. We feel incredibly privileged and humble to be involved in the World Cup again. It brings its own sense of momentous occasion.'

The World Cup had got underway on the Friday night with an immediate shock. Argentina had beaten tournament hosts France in Paris, and beaten them well. The French, already, would have their work cut out to make the knockout stages of their own World Cup. On the Saturday afternoon, both New Zealand and Australia had revealed their intentions by posting cricket scores against Italy and Japan respectively. Come Saturday evening and it was England's turn to put a rugby minnow in its place, or at least that was the plan.

In reality this never materialised. Just about the only positive thing to say about England's 28–10 victory over the USA was that it was, after all, a win, only England's second away from home in their past seventeen Test matches, and that there were no serious injuries picked up along the way.

The minuses, however, far outweighed the plusses. In scoring only three tries, England failed to secure a bonus point – gained for scoring four tries or losing by seven points or fewer – and ended the game very much on the back foot. To make matters worse, England faced the very real prospect of losing captain Phil Vickery for the crunch pool game against South Africa just six days later, having already probably lost Jonny Wilkinson to the ankle ligament injury that kept him out of this game. Vickery was expected to be cited for a trip on the American centre, Paul Emerick, which went unpunished by the South African referee Jonathan Kaplan. The New Zealand citing commissioner, Steve Hines, was looking at the incident late on the Saturday night after the game and England feared the worst.

The Webb Ellis Trophy stood glittering by the tunnel as the England players, led out by Josh Lewsey on the occasion of him winning his fiftieth cap, emerged to launch their defence of the World Cup. It was a timely reminder that, for all their pre-tournament problems, England were still champions. The problem, however, was that the spirited USA had not read the script.

While the England squad had negotiated a £2 million bonus should they retain the World Cup, the Americans – with a motley collection of professionals and amateurs – were on a £50 a day allowance. The bookmakers had this one down as an easy win for the world champions. Odds of 500-1-on were being bandied around, which was not surprising considering England beat the USA 106-8 in 1999, while what was effectively a third XV beat America 51-3 three months before this encounter. No wonder everyone was confident that England would hand out a good, old-fashioned thrashing in an old, coalmining town in the French region of Picardy.

An early Olly Barkley penalty was replied to in kind by Hercus. Then, within minutes of this, came a controversial moment. Hercus intercepted a pass from Ben Kay intended for Lewsey, ran half the length of the field and passed to Emerick, the outside centre, who was then felled by what appeared to be a trip by Vickery. Although the England captain's misdemeanour was missed by referee Kaplan, the US Eagles' and former Bristol coach, Peter Thorburn, was visibly angry. 'He stepped inside and it was an instinctive reaction,' Vickery would explain later. 'It was unfortunate but there was no malice on my part.'

England continued to make hard work of it. A second Barkley penalty took back the lead and for much of the first half they camped inside the American 22-metre line without much effect until the opposition inside centre, Vahafolau Esikia, was sent to the sin bin for using hands in the ruck. Barkley converted the resulting penalty and England finally crossed the American try-line when a Mike Catt chip to the corner gave Jason Robinson the chance to score. It had taken almost thirty-five minutes to unlock the American defence. Barkley scored England's second try in the dying seconds of the first half after Kay had provided the final pass following an attack started by a Lewsey burst.

The second half started slowly for England and America's scrum half, Chad Erskine, thought he had scored his country's first try of the tournament in the forty-eighth minute, only to be called back for a knock-on. Moments later, England finally produced some quality. Andrew Sheridan broke clear to produce a bullocking run. Then Tom Rees took a quick tap from a penalty and ran through three challenges to touch down, his first international try confirmed by Australian TV match official, Stuart Dickinson. It would not be the first time during this World Cup that Dickinson's video officiating would be called upon and, as England would discover, he would play a vital role in their story. For now, though, England would have expected the proverbial floodgates to open.

Instead, America held firm and, just after the hour, head coach Brian Ashton decided to throw on the cavalry. Vickery, Catt, Simon Shaw and Mark Regan all went off, and on came Matt Stevens, Andy Farrell, Martin Corry and George Chuter, but by then the rot had set in. With just over five minutes remaining, Lawrence Dallaglio was yellow-carded for killing the ball. From the resulting tap penalty the American reserve prop, Matekitonga Moeakiola, barrelled his way over the English line to be greeted by the loudest cheer of the night.

With the conversion from Hercus successful, the Eagles had

'The changing room is like a funeral right now'

Phil Vickery

managed to draw the second half 7-7. It had taken an amateur prop from the Park City Haggis Rugby Club in Utah to complete a less than satisfactory evening's work for England. Just about the only player to emerge positively from the whole affair was Olly Barkley, who was awarded man of the match for his personal tally of 18 points, including that try. All this after he was dumped on his head by American centre Paul Emerick after a crude spear tackle, unseen during the game, but the subject of another citing which would lead to a ban from the man who, ironically, was tripped by Vickery. 'Poor skill execution, poor communication, poor structure,' was Barkley's frank assessment of the England performance later.

To be fair to England, nobody was denying afterwards that this was far from the start England had been looking for at the World Cup. Phil Vickery's mood was, like his players, sombre when he met the world's assembled media one hour after the final whistle had blown.

'The changing room is like a funeral right now,' admitted England's captain. 'There's so much disappointment and so much frustration. We won the game, and we must give credit to America who made it hard for us, but people came and paid good money to see us and we've let a lot of people down. Now we'll have to accept the criticism that will come our way and just get on with it. Our performance tonight was not acceptable by our standards, and if we produce the same again versus South Africa in Paris on Friday we'll lose. It's as simple as that.'

Lawrence Dallaglio, like Vickery a 2003 World Cup winner, was equally frank in his assessment of the performance against the Eagles. Typically, though, he chose to be bullish about his team's prospects for the rest of the tournament. 'We won't play as badly as that again,' he predicted. When asked why he felt so confident

'Poor skill execution, poor communication, poor structure'

Olly Barkley

about making that promise he replied: 'Because we can't afford to do so. We have the players to dine at the top table of international rugby, but we're going to need a monumental display on Friday if we are to beat South Africa. It's fair to say we have lots of work to do in not an awful amount of time. From numbers one to fifteen we didn't have the energy or intensity we expected, we never settled, the breakdown was a mess, and it was a very ragged performance.

'It's pretty obvious we won't beat South Africa playing like that. Our basics let us down, and any misplaced kicks to the likes of Bryan Habana on Friday will result in major problems. We'll need to go up several levels, but I'm hoping the fear factor of facing the Springboks, the most physical side in the world, will give us the tonic we need. It could be worse, I suppose. We could be in France's position. If we beat South Africa then everyone's opinion will change. If we lose, then we'll be judged for what we are.'

Brian Ashton, looking shell-shocked after his first game in charge at a World Cup, attempted to look ahead, not back, on arguably the worst display of his short reign. 'There won't be any physical work this week but, mentally, we've got plenty to do,' he admitted. 'I'm hoping that facing the green and gold jerseys of South Africa will sharpen the senses. We'll spend the next twenty-four hours assessing the game and talking about selection. We've already prepared for the South Africa game, so there won't be much change in terms of what we've planned. Quite obviously, though, we're going to have to play a great deal better than that if we are to beat the Springboks. Today we achieved two out of our three objectives: we won the game and we suffered no injuries, but our display was not what we were looking for.'

Indeed it was not. South Africa would be waiting in six days' time in Paris and on this evidence the Springboks would be hot favourites to win.

Chapter 3: Pool Game
England v South Africa

Friday 14 September at the Stade de France, Paris
Attendance 77,000

ENGLAND 0		SOUTH AFRICA 36
Robinson	15	Montgomery
Lewsey	14	Pietersen
Noon	13	Fourie
Farrell	12	Steyn
Sackey	11	Habana
Catt	10	James
Perry	9	Du Preez
Sheridan	1	Du Randt
Regan	2	Smit (Captain)
Stevens	3	B.J.Botha
Shaw	4	Bakkies Botha
Kay	5	Matfield
Corry (Captain)	6	Van Heerden
Rees	7	Smith
Easter	8	Rossouw

Replacements

Gomarsall (for Perry) 41 mins	Muller (for Bakkies Botha) 53 mins
Moody (for Rees) 53 mins	Pienaar (for Habana) 56–60 mins
Borthwick (for Shaw) 55–60 mins	Pienaar (for Du Preez) 61 mins
Chuter (for Regan) 56 mins	Van Der Linde (for Du Randt) 61 mins
Tait (for Robinson) 58 mins	Du Plessis (for Smit) 70 mins
Borthwick (for Shaw) 77 mins	Skinstad (for Smith) 70 mins
Freshwater (for Sheridan) 77 mins	Pretorius (for James) 70 mins
Richards (for Noon) 79 mins	Olivier (for Steyn) 76 mins

Referee   J.Jutge (France)

England	South Africa
	Smith (try) 6 mins
	Montgomery (conversion) 7 mins
	Steyn (penalty) 11 mins
	Montgomery (penalty) 36 mins
	Pietersen (try) 38 mins
	Montgomery (conversion) 39 mins
	Montgomery (penalty) 46 mins
	Montgomery (penalty) 55 mins
	Pietersen (try) 64 mins
	Montgomery (conversion) 64 mins
	Montgomery (penalty) 79 mins

Match statistics

England		South Africa
0	Tries	3
0	Conversions	3
(0) 0	Penalties (taken)	5 (5)
0	Drop goals	0
8	Scrums won	5
1	Scrums lost	4
16	Lineouts won	12
3	Lineouts lost	3
1	Turnovers won	9
49	Tackles made	86
8	Tackles lost	14
1	Line breaks	4
58%	Possession	42%
50%	Territory	50%
12	Errors	10
29	Possession kicked	35
8	Penalties conceded	6
6'43"	Time in oppo 22	5'34"
0	Yellow cards	0
0	Red cards	0

England v South Africa Record

Overall	Played 28	England won 12	South Africa won 16	Drawn 1
World Cup	Played 3	England won 1	South Africa won 2	

The way England under-performed in their World Cup opener was not the only issue concerning the team management when they woke up on the Sunday morning back in their Versailles hotel. There had been no news concerning whether captain Phil Vickery would be cited or not after his trip on Paul Emerick and nobody was quite sure, with the citing deadline on Monday evening, whether no news was good or bad news.

At least the US Eagles had declined their right to refer the incident to Steve Hinds, the match citing commissioner from New Zealand. This, however, did not guarantee that Hinds would adopt a similar view. It would all depend on whether he felt Vickery's offence deserved a red card. If he did, then the prop would almost certainly be banned for at least the South Africa game, and possibly for longer. If he did not, then Vickery would be free to face the Springboks.

Previous cases pointed favourably towards the Wasps player. France's Christophe Dominici received a yellow card for tripping Jason Robinson in the World Cup semi-final back in 2003; while Serge Betsen, who broke Stuart Abbott's leg during a Heineken Cup tie, was first cited and then acquitted. The England team and management could only wait.

They did not wait long, however. On the Monday Hinds duly cited England's captain, stating that in his view the offence did, indeed, warrant a red card, and the England camp prepared for another likely setback. Unless Vickery was going to be lucky, it looked as if he would be facing a two-week ban at best, and possibly up to four weeks, the latter making him eligible only for the semi-final onwards which, on the back of England's display against America, seemed like a pipedream. It would mean England, who had had their fill of changes the previous week, having to reconstruct their front row, with Matt Stevens, formerly an

Under-21 Springbok before moving to Bath and switching allegiances, next in line to take over at tight-head. There would also have to be a new captain appointed and, despite having the likes of Wilkinson, Catt, Dallaglio and Robinson in the squad, Martin Corry was the slight favourite to take over the armband.

All would be revealed on the Tuesday afternoon, after Vickery and Richard Smith QC, the lawyer added to Clive Woodward's backroom staff during the 2003 World Cup, had attended a hearing at the Place Vendôme offices of the legal firm Clifford Chance in Paris. The case would be heard by Professor Lorne Crerar, a prominent Scottish lawyer with a recent track record of tough action on international players found guilty of violent conduct. It was Smith who helped England four years previously when they escaped with a £10,000 fine after fielding sixteen players for thirty seconds during a confusing substitution against Samoa, plus a touchline ban for fitness coach Dave Reddin.

While England braced themselves for the news, on the Monday evening one or two in the camp admitted that thoughts during the America fixture may have been wandering towards the Springboks. 'I hate to say it but we are all human and I suspect quite a few guys would have had their minds on what happens next week,' said forwards coach John Wells.

Jason Robinson underlined this point. 'No disrespect to the USA, but everyone has been waiting for this game,' he added. 'Nobody expects us to win, except the guys in the England squad. Let's bring it on and get into them.'

> 'No disrespect to the USA, but everyone has been waiting for this game'
>
> *Jason Robinson*

All was not perfect in the South African camp, either. Jean de Villiers tore his left bicep during the side's defeat of Samoa on the Sunday afternoon, and was returning home to undergo surgery. The centre was substituted early in the second half and taken to hospital for x-rays. He had also missed the 2003 World Cup through injury.

It was, however, just about the only setback in an otherwise satisfactory last couple of weeks for the South Africans. They came to France on the back of a convincing 3-27 win at Murrayfield in a warm-up Test against a virtually full-strength Scotland side, and followed that up with a 59-7 thrashing of Samoa in the first pool game, which featured four tries from winger Bryan Habana. No wonder they spoke of the forthcoming Test against England with confidence.

'If we play well there should be no reason why we won't win the game,' said their head coach, Jake White. 'I know it was a depleted English side in South Africa a couple of months ago but we've beaten them three times out of the last four and we were unlucky at Twickenham last November in that one defeat. I wouldn't say Friday's game is do-or-die, in the sense that the loser won't be eliminated, but winning your pool is essential to a successful World Cup. That's why it's such an important game. England have obviously gone back to what worked well for them in 2003. They have gone for a huge pack of forwards, a pair of half backs who can kick and inside centres that can hold the ball close and keep the forwards in the game. But there is a real belief and confidence in our team. They have been waiting four years for this.'

So, too, had Eddie Jones, the former Australia coach who saw his side defeated by England in Sydney in the 2003 World Cup final. Subsequently, he had lost his position at the Australian Rugby Union, but the Wallabies' loss was South Africa's gain. Four years on and Jones could be found in the green and gold of a Springbok track-suit in his role as Jake White's technical assistant, which he held on a part-time basis shared with Saracens, where he also acted as a consultant.

As far as White was concerned Jones was 'worth his weight in gold'. Few could disagree that having Jones onside could only be an advantage. 'Eddie is a very astute rugby man who adds a huge amount of value in terms of analysing all opposition teams,' White would continue to say. 'He knows our strengths and our weaknesses and his technical expertise is immense. On top of that, his other great advantage is that he has been to a World Cup final. He knows all about the psychology at that very highest level, what works in semi-finals and finals, and what doesn't. He understands the psyche of the World Cup and probably knows where he made mistakes. In that respect he brings the benefit of hindsight. Not only does he work in the English set-up, he has various Australian connections at several English clubs. At a World Cup you need as much information on the opposition as you can get.'

White was an impressive figure, a worldly wise coach who learnt his apprenticeship under Nick Mallett with the Springboks back at the 1999 World Cup. His captain, John Smit, who played in that pool game defeat in Perth to England in 2003, was an equally intelligent presence. He had no qualms admitting that his South African team had modelled their World Cup campaign on England's successful operation four years previously, in a bid to wipe out their bitter memories of that tournament. Smit, who had played in a record forty-five Tests as captain, had guided South Africa to those two thumping wins over England three months earlier, and was determined to stop his side suffering the same fate as their previous team four years ago. He had done his homework thoroughly for this World Cup, in particular studying England, their players, their matches, and their previous World Cup encounters in readiness for the probable group-deciding clash that week. South Africa had even employed Sherylle Calder, the vision expert brought in by Clive Woodward in 2003. Now she, too, was wearing the green and gold.

'There is much to learn from our games with England,' Smit, a twenty-nine-year-old from Pietersburg, explained. 'And there is much to learn from how England went about their business in 2003. I played in that game then and I remember that, for thirty minutes, there was nothing between the teams. Maybe we even

'There is much to learn from our games with England'

John Smit

had a slight edge. Then England scored a try out of the blue [Will Greenwood from Lewis Moody's charge-down] and everything changed. Their winning habit kicked in. Sherylle has told us to be prepared for unseen circumstances. International rugby is all about fine margins. Four years ago our whole preparation was geared towards that England game. It was a big mistake. We should have taken a leaf out of England's book and looked no further than the next game.'

The architect behind that Springbok defeat, Clive Woodward, spoke up in support of the current England team as they prepared to face South Africa in the World Cup once more. 'We have the players to beat South Africa,' insisted the 2003 World Cup-winning coach. 'I know we have. I know the players. The one team which has always had an Indian sign over South Africa is England. They can win this game and go all the way like four years ago. It's fifty-fifty. Win and the World Cup will take off. Lose and it will be very difficult, but it's not all doom and gloom. These are one-offs. People said we'd get beaten by France in the one semi-final four years ago and everyone said New Zealand would beat Australia in the other.'

The Tuesday before the South Africa international ended up far worse than anyone had imagined, and most people within the camp were already bracing themselves for a testing day. Vickery, as expected, received a two-match ban, which meant he would be unavailable for the clash with the Springboks, and the game the following Saturday against Samoa, which England could ill afford to lose. It could have been worse. At least the England captain was spared a four-week ban, but for the proud, patriotic prop, it was the worst possible start to the World Cup campaign and the personal responsibility he felt was huge. Professor Crerar classified Vickery's action 'a deliberate act delivered with some force, causing the opposing player to be knocked over.' Under the rules this was classed as a mid-entry offence which carried a maximum punishment of four weeks. The maximum fifty per cent reduction was then applied, with a number of mitigating circumstances taken into account. 'These include the player's immediate admission of culpability, his good character and conduct during the hearing.'

Ironically, South Africa's influential open-side flanker, Schalk Burger, was also banned, this time for four matches, after a dangerous tackle against Samoa went unpunished. There were some who may have felt the bans evened each other out, but there was no doubt England needed Vickery's influence a great deal more than South Africa, with their magnificent strength in depth, required the blond flanker's services. In another twist, American centre Paul Emerick, the victim of Vickery's trip, received a five-week suspension for his spear tackle on Olly Barkley. It prompted Nigel Melville, speaking as president and chief executive of American rugby, to make an angry response. 'As an Englishman I am not complaining that Vickery's got two weeks,' he said. 'Phil was caught off balance and it was a natural thing to put his foot out and try to stop a try being scored against his team. But I'm amazed at Emerick's ban.'

In England's current state, perhaps worse news even than Vickery's ban was the sight of Barkley pulling up during training with a damaged hip muscle. With Wilkinson quite clearly struggling to pass himself fit for South Africa, this was the worst event to hit England. If Barkley, too, was out for the Springboks clash, then England would have to turn to Andrew Farrell, and this was a man, for all his conversions kicked in rugby league, who had managed three points-scoring kicks for Saracens in two years of playing rugby union. Indeed, the last time he had kicked a goal at Test match level was for the Great Britain rugby league team against Australia in 2004. Now it was likely he would be called upon to kick for England in a game in which any points scored would be crucial. Named as substitute cover for the fly half and

'You can only practise and do your best'

Andrew Farrell

inside centre positions Farrell had at least upped his kicking practice since Wilkinson's injury and he, unlike everyone else, remained unflustered.

'You can only practise and do your best,' was his laid-back way of approaching the forthcoming demands likely to be placed upon him. 'If you miss, you're a villain. If you kick them all, you're a hero. You've got to be prepared to take the rough with the smooth. I've been in situations like this before and the best thing is not even to think about it but just get on with it and try to enjoy the occasion. The balls being used for the tournament seem to be lighter than those we use at home in the Premiership but it's the same for everybody. The more I practise, the more comfortable I feel. We'll have to see what happens and how Olly is, but I'm quite relaxed about it.'

The alternative to Farrell was Catt, who had also kicked plenty of goals for England in the dim and distant past, but had not taken a single conversion for London Irish during the previous season. It was likely, if Barkley and Wilkinson failed to make it, that the mercurial Catt would start at fly half, with Farrell outside him in the number twelve jersey, even though Catt, two days shy of his thirty-sixth birthday come Friday night, had not started an international in this position since the famous English defeat by Wales at Wembley Stadium in 1999!

Brian Ashton was on the verge of pulling out what remaining hair he still had after this latest setback. He named Barkley in the England starting XV for South Africa regardless, in the hope that by the end of the week the Bath player would be fit, but he could not hide his frustration at seeing a second stand off fall in the most innocuous of fashions.

'Olly was just running around,' Ashton said. 'There was nobody anywhere near him. It was the usual England injury. You could have understood it better if he'd been on the floor with ten people kicking the hell out of him. A decision will be made in the next twenty-four hours whether he will be fit to play on Friday night or not. If Olly is not fit and Jonny becomes fit then the problem is solved. I'll see what the doctor says.'

For the time being, Barkley remained in the team but such was the confusing state of England's selection for the South Africa game that the seventh and last reserve picked came under the name of A.N.Other.

The idea before the start of the World Cup was to select more or less the same side for at least the first two games, such was the quick turnaround in games, but so poor was England's display against the United States that this theory was demolished by Ashton and his management team. The main casualties were Lawrence Dallaglio, Mark Cueto and Joe Worsley, who went from the starting XV against the Eagles to not even making the bench against the Springboks, despite Mr A.N.Other. They were replaced by Nick Easter, Paul Sackey and Martin Corry respectively, with Sackey playing on the left wing and Robinson reverting to full back in place of Cueto whom Ashton admitted 'struggled to find his form, possibly due to a groin niggle' against America.

Sackey had the little matter of marking Bryan Habana, the South African winger who began his World Cup campaign with four sparkling tries against Samoa. Before the start of the tournament he raced against a cheetah back home in South Africa in a publicity stunt, and only narrowly lost. Sackey, a 10.7 second 100 metre runner when at school, had been training with sprint coach Margot Wells, the wife of the 1980 Olympic 100 metres champion Allan Wells, and didn't seem overly concerned by his latest challenge. 'I haven't found any cheetahs in London,' said the Wasps man. 'Habana is an awesome player but I'm not too worried about him. I'll worry about myself and concentrate on what I need to do.'

> ## 'I haven't found any cheetahs in London'
>
> *Paul Sackey*

The England management were considering appealing against Vickery's ban but, for the time being at least, he was also out and in came Matt Stevens instead, who had the chance to add some rugby fame to the celebrity status he required when finishing as runner up on TV's *Celebrity X Factor* programme earlier in the year.

By the Wednesday night, just forty-eight hours before the big kick-off, Barkley had been ruled out, with Wilkinson almost certain to follow, and Farrell had been named, at least initially, at fly half, with Catt, confusingly, outside him. This was the biggest match England would face since the World Cup final in 2003 and yet England had little option but to turn to a Farrell–Catt axis, with the latter planning to alternate positions with the former rugby league star. It was a toss-up, for all their experience, to know which of the two would be better suited to play outside Shaun Perry at ten. Farrell's experience as a rugby union stand off amounted to one appearance for the Saracens 'A' team that season; Catt would need to play it through memory. It was hardly the best preparation to face the might of the Springboks.

Still, at least Rob Andrew, England's elite director of rugby, backed England's latest number ten, and Andrew knew a thing or two about playing in that position. 'This is a wonderful opportunity for Andy to prove to his doubters what a great player he is,' said Andrew. 'If any one man ever had the opportunity to show exactly what he's made of, then Andy has it now. In terms of kicking goals, he has kicked many pressure goals in rugby league and I'd imagine two-point pressure kicks are the same as the three-point ones. This is one of the biggest challenges this group of players will have faced. I believe they will respond.'

England responded to the lack of Vickery for the next two games by summoning Bristol prop Darren Crompton as cover, calling him on his thirty-fifth birthday to announce the surprising news. 'If we lose another prop between now and kick-off against South Africa then, technically, under International Board rules, we could not field a team,' Andrew explained.

The other news from a packed day was the confirmation that Corry would, once again, take over the captaincy. The big Leicester forward did not believe he would ever take the English helm again after losing the leadership to Vickery following England's November defeat to South Africa at Twickenham, a result that cost previous head coach Andy Robinson his job, but now the armband was his again, such are the nuances of international rugby union.

It was all pretty confusing even on the day before the kick-off. Catt and Farrell, so it transpired, would now be wearing the number ten and twelve jerseys in that order, although the latter was being described as an 'auxiliary fly half'.

Catt, true to form, refused to hide behind the fact that it was hardly the best way to go into an international of such enormity. 'We've had one team run and that's about it,' he admitted. 'It's not much, is it? Unfortunately, we haven't had time for any more. It's about understanding where we want to go and how we want to get there. Faz and I have to control the game. As the main decision-makers it's up to us to make sure we give the team the necessary direction. We know it's a big ask, especially after the last three performances. The errors made against America have got to be wiped out, otherwise Bryan Habana and the rest will destroy us. We are massive underdogs but we know we will give it a real thrash.'

In the face of such adversity head coach Ashton sensed a stiffening of resolve. 'There is a mood within this squad which I've not seen since I took over in January,' he said. 'There's an atmosphere I've not felt before. Now we have to reproduce that when we get out on to the field.' Asked if he believed the Catt–Farrell partnership would work, he responded in bullish fashion. 'If I didn't feel they could do it, I wouldn't put them there,' Ashton said. Typically, he tried to add a little humour to the catalogue of mishaps that had hit him and his team during the week. 'I looked up at the clear blue sky first thing this morning and thought there's probably a piano some-where up there waiting to come down on me.'

The last words, aptly, were down to Martin Corry. He had been part of the 2003 World Cup-winning squad, albeit as a bit-part player rather than a key figure, but he believed the forthcoming game against South Africa dwarfed any-thing he had been involved with

'So much is riding on this game that I do think it's bigger than anything else I've been involved in'

Martin Corry

before. 'So much is riding on this game that I do think it's bigger than anything else I've been involved in,' he admitted. A player's player, if ever there was one, there was nothing he relished more than facing a task of such enormity.

'We will draw strength from adversity and we've certainly had our fair share of that over the past few days,' said Corry. 'It's had the effect of pulling us all closer together. We will take motivation from wherever we can. In terms of reuniting the squad, this has been great. As far as I'm concerned the ideal game for us in the cir-cumstances has to be South Africa. Kick-off at nine o'clock tomor-row night cannot come soon enough. We've had the rollickings earlier in the week, and rightly so. We deserved them. We let our-selves down, our supporters down, and our country down.

'If that American game had to happen to make us realise where we were going wrong, then it will not have been in vain. We've said a lot of things and we all know how easy talking is. Now it's all about generating all the emotion and belief into this one match. It's down to every individual now. Do we lie back and feel sorry for ourselves? Definitely not. Come Saturday morning, nobody's going to say: "Never mind, the situation wasn't ideal." We have a Test match to win and that's all that concerns us. Hopefully, we are going to put a lot of wrongs right.'

The theory sounded good, but in fact the practice turned out somewhat differently. Whatever England may have dreamt about on Thursday night, come Friday night it turned into the kind of nightmare to wake you up in cold sweats for many years to come. There have been a few bad times before in the World Cup but never before, in the twenty-year history of the tournament, had England been embarrassed to the extent they were by South Africa. No points, not even a meaningful attempt at the goal, and major injuries to boot. A 36-0 defeat represented the lowest ebb England had reached in a very long time.

The only ray of light was provided by full back Jason Robinson who, at times, appeared to be taking on the Springboks by himself. Utterly fearless under the high ball that rained down on him repeatedly from the black night's sky, he was also scintillating in attack, when only his running darts appeared to trouble South Africa. It was Robinson who scored England's only try in the 2003 World Cup final, and the former rugby league star had come out of retirement to help England defend their crown. However, it seemed to everyone in the 77,000 crowd that his tournament had come to a premature end when he pulled up on the attack in the second half with what looked like a painful hamstring tear.

It summed up England's torrid evening. And it summed up their up-and-down history with South Africa. It was the Springboks who were the last to hold the English to a scoreless sheet when they beat them 18-0 during the 1998 Tour of Hell, and it was also South Africa who had previously inflicted England's heaviest ever World Cup defeat, when Jannie De Beer's five drop goals in the 1999 quarter-final helped them to a convincing 44-21 victory.

Since then England had gained some kind of revenge by beating them in the pool stages of the 2003 World Cup, a result that consigned South Africa to a quarter-final defeat to New Zealand while England went on to become world champions. Now the pendulum had swung, and this time violently, back towards the South Africans.

In truth England hardly helped themselves. Too much possession was kicked away down South African throats, and with nine turnovers also resulting in lost possession, it gave the Springboks numerous chances to launch attacks, something they did with relish.

The portents had not been good before the kick-off. A combination of the previous, contrasting weekend displays and the chaotic English preparation for this encounter meant that it was always going to be a tough ask to fend off the Springboks, but a good start would have helped.

Instead, England were 10 points down inside the first eleven minutes. First J.P. (Jon-Paul) Pietersen set off on a blindside run to make a good 30 metres before sending the impressive Fourie du Preez away. The scrum half, who would later, and deservedly, be awarded man of the match, almost made it to the line before a Robinson ankle-tap brought him down. He was down but he was not held and a simple pass to Juan Smith saw the flanker touch down in the seventh minute.

All eyes had been on Bryan Habana before and during this game. The rapid winger had labelled his intent the week before with those four tries against Samoa, and England were desperate not to provide him with any space. The problem was, though, that Pietersen was no mug on the other wing, and it was his exploitation of space that helped give South Africa the perfect start.

Two penalties from Francois Steyn, the precocious youngster with the big boot on him, and Percy Montgomery increased South Africa's lead and the game was, most likely, already over when the Springboks scored their second try just before the break. It was a score that would have had England head coach Brian Ashton, and especially defence coach Mike Ford, shaking their heads in bewilderment. South Africa dropped turnover ball but England's overeager midfield came up so quickly that du Preez saw only empty space between him and the English line some 60 metres away. Swooping on the ball the scrum half almost made it to the line but, like the first try, fell metres short. J.P.Pietersen was there to finish off the move, touching down close enough to the posts for the unflappable Montgomery to convert. Half time and already 20-0 down. Only a brave man could predict anything other than a substantial Springbok victory.

In his half-time talk Ashton made references to the 'Rumble in the Jungle', the heavyweight world boxing bout between champion George Foreman and challenger Muhammad Ali in former Zaire. In what went down as one of the greatest of sporting comebacks ever, Ali allowed Foreman to punch him at will for the first five rounds until the big champion tired, then sprang from the ropes to knock him out. It was, back in 1973, a sensation, but there was no danger of any 'rope-a-dope' repeat in Paris thirty-four years on.

Instead, South Africa took the early second-half points thanks to two further penalties from Montgomery. He would end the night with four. With his long, blond locks and pretty boy features, the Springbok full back had taken his fair share of stick over his long and distinguished career, but he would never play better than he did during the 2007 World Cup. By then Andy Gomarsall had come on to replace Shaun Perry, who had endured a miserable night at the hands of opposing scrum half du Preez. Lewis Moody came on to replace Tom Rees, then Steve Borthwick came on as a blood bin replacement for Simon Shaw, and George Chuter for Mark Regan.

In the fifty-eighth minute, Matthew Tait was asked to leave the bench and replace Robinson after the full back, in attacking flow, seized up and went crashing down. The injury looked so serious it appeared as if a sniper had fired a shot at his leg from the stands. Later, Robinson's experience and intelligence would become apparent. By stopping running immediately, and hitting the deck, he had given himself another chance, but at the time, on a desperate night for English rugby, it seemed to all the world that a great career in both codes of rugby had just come to a sorry end. That's what the 77,000 crowd concluded as they rose from their seats in applause to see him hobble off the pitch. And that's what many of the South African players believed, too, as they showed their respect for a brilliant foe by clapping him or patting him on the back as he made his exit from the pitch.

The game was already lost by then, but South Africa, given the rare opportunity to humiliate England, stuck the knife further in. Late on that man du Preez was at it again, switching to the right of a ruck and creating so much space in the process that his pass gave Pietersen a simple run in for his second try of the night. There was still time for Jamie Noon to leave the proceedings on a stretcher before French referee, Joel Jutge, put England out of their misery by blowing for full time. In between his first whistle and his last South Africa had enjoyed total control. It had been, indisputably, the worst display put up by defending world champions in the history of the tournament. No wonder England hurried to the relative sanctity of their dressing room, while the jubilant South Africans embarked on a lap of honour.

Martin Corry, England's stand-in captain for the banned Phil Vickery, looked stunned afterwards as Friday night turned into the early hours of Saturday morning. He had dealt with some harsh blows over the years following the 2003 tournament, but none was more painful than this one. 'The lads are shell-shocked,' he reported. 'We went into the game expecting to win but we gifted them twenty points and we were playing catch-up against one of the best sides in the world. We're not going to hit the self-destruct button because of the challenge facing us next week. It may be difficult for you to believe, but we think we can hit our potential and when we do, you will see a different performance. We have to keep striving to produce the performance we know we are capable of.'

Brian Ashton refused to concede that this was a worse display even than against the minnows of

'The lads are shell-shocked'

Martin Corry

America six days earlier. 'I won't accept it was a worse perform-ance,' he insisted. 'South Africa are one of the top two sides in the world and they played extremely well for eighty minutes. I thought their kicking game was outstanding. By half time the game was over. We had a go at our guys, which was fully justified, and some of the individual play showed up much better in the sec-ond half, but if we'd played as we had the previous week we'd have shipped eighty points.'

Nevertheless, any repeat of either of their first two perform-ances in the World Cup against the following week's opponents, Samoa, and England, the defending world champions, would become the first title-holders to be knocked out of the tournament in the group stages. It was a point reinforced by Jake White. 'England will have to play much better to beat Samoa,' said the South African head coach. 'To be honest, my players are sitting in the dressing room saying that the Samoans were much more phys-ical opponents than the English.'

It was difficult to know what was worse: the accusation that Samoa presented a bigger challenge to his team than the English, or the fact that White, a serious Anglophile and admirer of English rugby, expressed his remorse for the plight of England. 'England are world champions, after all,' he reasoned. 'They are a power-house rugby nation. Nobody likes to see them at such a low ebb. We were really worried about this game, but I know what it's like for them now because I've been there myself with South Africa. The only way for them is up.'

One by one the depressed English players emerged from their own dressing room both bemused and incredulous about what had just happened. There was one thing they were certain about, however. One more defeat, and Samoa were capable of inflicting such a setback on the evidence so far provided in this tournament, and England would be leaving the World Cup early.

Mike Catt, never one to shirk away from the truth, spelled out the grim reality of the situation he and his team-mates found

'We've got to raise our game by a significant amount or we'll be on the plane home'

Tom Rees

themselves in. 'Everyone predicted all week that South Africa would beat us convincingly and I've got to say they've all been spot on,' conceded the centre. 'Absolutely nothing worked for us. I'd love to be able to talk about what we're going to do to get it right for next week. I can say we'll be intense, we won't repeat the display we've just produced and we'll be up for it, but I said all that last week after the United States game and this is the result. I don't really have any answers right now, except to say it's very possible Samoa will beat us next week.'

Josh Lewsey, normally bullish even in defeat and, like Catt, a World Cup winner just four years previously, was also lost for any clues as to where England went next. 'It's easy to point to things that have not gone our way,' said the winger. 'We've had injuries, we lost our captain to a citing, we've had last-minute changes in formations, and everything else, but there are no excuses for this at all. We just didn't perform. It's difficult to explain why this is, just as it's difficult to work out how we're going to improve. It's pretty obvious Samoa will beat us unless we play better – a lot better.'

No other England player disagreed with this. 'There's no point dressing it up,' said flanker Tom Rees. 'And there's no escaping the fact. We've got to raise our game by a significant amount or we'll be on the plane home. The ability and the experience we have shouldn't be questioned, but maybe we don't quite believe it ourselves.'

Nick Easter, who took over from Lawrence Dallaglio in the No. 8 berth for this match, was with his back row colleague Rees on this. 'Samoa can clearly beat us after we've produced three poor displays in a row,' Easter said, referring to the last warm-up game in Marseille against France, as well as USA and now South Africa in the World Cup. 'They caused South Africa a lot more problems than we did, and it's going to be a tough challenge now to beat them. What was worse? Conceding thirty-six points and three tries, or being nilled? Frankly I'd say neither makes good reading but I'd say being nilled is the ultimate embarrassment for us. It was a proper trouncing.'

Full marks for honesty, at least, and over the next few days a good many more harsh truths would be spoken as England's date with destiny, in the large, brooding shape of Samoa, loomed disturbingly on the horizon.

Chapter 4: England v Samoa

Saturday 22 September at the Stade de la Beaujoire, Nantes   *Attendance* 38,000

ENGLAND 44		SAMOA 22
Lewsey	15	Crichton
Sackey	14	Lemi
Tait	13	Mapusua
Barkley	12	Lima
Cueto	11	A.Tuilagi
Wilkinson	10	Fuimaono-Sapolu
Gomarsall	9	Polu
Sheridan	1	Lealamanua
Chuter	2	Schwalger
Stevens	3	Johnston
Shaw	4	Tekori
Kay	5	Thompson
(Captain) Corry	6	Leo
Worsley	7	Sititi (Captain)
Easter	8	H.Tuilagi

Replacements

Freshwater (for Sheridan) 65 mins
Borthwick (for Shaw) 65 mins
Moody (for Worsley) 70 mins
Hipkiss (for Tait) 73 mins

Palaamo (for Lealamanua) 62 mins
So'oialo (for Polu) 67 mins
Vaeluaga (for H.Tuilagi) 70 mins
Meafou (for Mapusua) 70 mins
Lui (for Lima) 73 mins
Purdie (for Tekori) 75 mins
Lealamanua (for Johnston) 75 mins

Referee   A.Lewis (Ireland)

Scorers

England	Samoa
Corry (try) 2 mins	Crichton (penalty) 9 mins
Wilkinson (conversion) 3 mins	Crichton (penalty) 12 mins
Wilkinson (drop goal) 6 mins	Crichton (penalty) 38 mins
Wilkinson (penalty) 15 mins	Crichton (penalty) 40 mins
Wilkinson (penalty) 22 mins	Crichton (penalty) 42 mins
Sackey (try) 32 mins	Polu (try) 47 mins
Wilkinson (conversion) 33 mins	Crichton (conversion) 48 mins
Wilkinson (penalty) 45 mins	
Wilkinson (drop goal) 69 mins	
Wilkinson (penalty) 72 mins	
Corry (try) 76 mins	
Wilkinson (conversion) 77 mins	
Sackey (try) 80 mins	

Match statistics

England		Samoa
4	Tries	1
3	Conversions	1
(6) 4	Penalties (taken)	5 (5)
2	Drop goals	0
5	Scrums won	9
0	Scrums lost	1
8	Lineouts won	9
1	Lineouts lost	5
4	Turnovers won	3
54	Tackles made	85
11	Tackles lost	24
1	Line breaks	1
57%	Possession	43%
54%	Territory	46%
6	Errors	6
36	Possession kicked	23
5	Penalties conceded	7
6'53"	Time in oppo 22	5'55"
0	Yellow cards	0
0	Red cards	0

England v Samoa Record

Overall	Played 5	England won 5
World Cup	Played 3	England won 3

The recriminations following the South African debacle continued over the weekend and into the start of England's most important week since the 2003 World Cup. England spent the Saturday and Sunday recovering from their physical exertions, and trying to restore some belief in themselves and the squad. Samoa, their next opponents, lost their South Seas derby game with Tonga 15-19 in a brutal battle and, like England, would need to win the following Saturday just to stay in the tournament. If England were to succeed – and that seemed a big 'if' after Friday night's capitulation to the Springboks – they would then need to face a Tongan team on a high. It wasn't appearing to be getting any easier.

To underline this fact, Jamie Noon, last seen being stretchered off the Stade de France pitch late on in the game on the Friday night, was told his damaged knee spelt the end of the World Cup for him. He returned home to Newcastle on the Monday and his club team-mate, Toby Flood, unlucky to miss the final World Cup squad selection cut in the first place, would be flying out to replace him. It was ironic that as Flood, a fine kicker in his own right, was arriving in France, Jonny Wilkinson was confident he would have fully recovered from his twisted ankle in time for the clash with Samoa. From having to ask Andrew Farrell to be the principal kicker against South Africa, which was hardly ideal given his lack of match practice in union, England were now spoilt for choice.

As it turned out, Farrell was never even asked to kick at goal, such was the paucity of English possession and the discipline of the Springboks on the pitch to prevent penalty chances close to goal until the game was won and lost. England's defence coach, Mike Ford, hardly shed a ray of positive light on the Andrew Farrell experiment, either, when he assessed what had gone wrong.

'Opponents may be technically better at the moment. I wouldn't argue with that.'

Mike Ford

'Twelve months out of the game have done Andy Farrell no favours,' said Ford. 'He's getting to grips with it, but it's probably just a bit too late at his age to be where he wants to be. We use him as best we can. He is a great leader in terms of his talk and presence but it's not as simple as saying we are not using Faz as best we can. We have to look at the bigger picture. As it stands, it has not worked out for us as a team.'

Farrell was not the only player Ford and his fellow coaches were finding out about. 'We think we get selection right every time but, as the tournament unfolds, we are still finding out about players performing under intense pressure. It's not a case of not knowing our best XV, but we were disappointed with our game management against South Africa. We are where we are with some players and that's no disrespect to anyone. We just haven't got these sort of world-class players in our team. In 2003, everyone would agree we had six or seven players who would have got into any world XV. I'm not sure how many would get in now. I'm not saying they're not great players. It's just that maybe other teams have overtaken us. Opponents may be technically better at the moment. I wouldn't argue with that.

'Physically, I think we're OK but I want to see more pace. I really did believe we were up for the game last Friday night. We were on the edge in the warm-up and you cannot criticise the players for effort. There was a lot of anger and embarrassment afterwards. My stomach's in turmoil because coaches go through the emotional wringer as well. The way the team played made it very difficult to execute our game plan. We got our kicks wrong. Mike Catt has not played at number ten in an international for a long time. You can't just step in there and expect a first-class performance from him. We lost our two pivotal tens and it's difficult to execute what we wanted.'

The mood was hardly lightened with the state of Jason Robinson, either. The Sale Shark was staying on in the England camp and, according to an England medical bulletin, 'entering an accelerated hamstring rehabilitation period,' but few believed he would be seen again on a rugby pitch in this World Cup or, indeed, ever as he was due to retire after the tournament.

At least Ford remained defiant. 'People are calling us underdogs against Samoa, but Martin Corry has never been an underdog in his life and neither has Jonny Wilkinson and a few others,' he said. 'What we can hopefully do is get a little bit of confidence, get a win by whatever means and get some momentum going into the Tonga match. We can beat Samoa, we can beat Tonga and then we've got a quarter-final. We're going to give it our best and give a performance against Samoa so people will be able to say: "Maybe England can do something in this tournament."'

There were plenty of others happy to offer their views concerning what had gone wrong with English rugby, and most of them were Antipodean. Eddie Jones, the Wallaby head coach now working as South Africa's technical assistant, reckoned relegation and promotion in the English leagues inhibited player development. 'The tendency in England with such matters at stake is to be conservative, whereas in the Super 14, where relegation does not exist, you play the younger guys to give them experience. In England they always go back to experience and I think a performance like that against South Africa last Friday has been coming for a while. Two coaches in the past three years has been disruptive, so there are extenuating circumstances, but what they have failed to do since Andy Robinson went is to stick to a style. They have changed between one and another and, though you might get short-term relief from that, you get no medium- or long-term development.'

John Connolly, the current Australian head coach, agreed. 'Everyone knows about the club versus country issue and there is a growing awareness that some clubs are shying away from field-ing English players,' said Connolly, who knows a thing or two about English rugby, having preceded Brian Ashton as head coach at Bath. 'Players coming through, maybe going straight from school to a Premiership club, find a gap. Maybe a youngster in the development XV meets a Simon Shaw coming back from an injury, maybe he's overlooked for an overseas player. The structure of the game affects the kind of game you play, as well. If it's not for the domestic title, or the Premiership play-offs, or a European place, it's to avoid relegation. There's just so much at stake on every game and that can inhibit players and coaches.'

That said, Connolly predicted that England would bounce back well against Samoa. 'England have a scrum, they have a lineout, Jonny Wilkinson should be back, and they therefore have the abil-ity to play very well,' he added. 'I don't think England are weak at all. What they have had is a number of disruptions. They imploded under the pressure of South Africa's game and, remem-ber, the Springboks are a brutal side. I wouldn't be writing the English off just yet.' They would be words which would later be extremely relevant to Connolly and his Australian players.

On the Monday, nearly three thousand schoolchildren, given the afternoon off from school, gathered to watch England's belea-guered troops go back to work. They greeted thirty-sixth birthday boy Mike Catt with a quick rendition of 'Happy Birthday'. By then Jason Robinson was able to jog, albeit gingerly, around the perimeter of the England training pitch in Versailles close to their hotel. The winger-cum-full back was in good form despite his injury setback that still seemed to have ended his tournament prematurely. A former England cap-tain, of course, and the man who scored England's only try in the 2003 World Cup final, even from the physio's bed he was issuing out defiant messages.

'We are in the trenches'

Jason Robinson

'We are in the trenches,' Robinson said. 'Those who take the field in the next match simply have to do it. It starts with every individual. You can have the best coach in the world and the best trainer but, in the end, it's all down to the players on the field. We have to take all the criticism on the chin because we deserve it and we will keep getting it until we find the right performance. I've been saying for the last three weeks that there is a performance waiting to come out but I'm sick of saying the same thing. If we don't win against Samoa, we are going home early, for sure.

'It was such a shame we didn't come up with a performance last weekend because what a great atmosphere all those England supporters made. They will have been very disappointed but we need everyone behind us and the more who do that, the better it will be. There's still hope.' For him, as well? 'I'm optimistic that I'll feature, but we'll need a couple of wins first,' he answered. 'I've certainly not given up.'

Brian Ashton, too, was in a far more positive mood after spending a miserable first few hours of Saturday morning trying to work out what had gone wrong. A squad meeting had been called later that morning and everyone present, from players to management, was invited to air their views. It later emerged that this is exactly what took place, and the views aired were full and frank. The players were frustrated and said so. They were not happy with what they were being asked to do, and not happy with the way in which their confusion had spilled out into their match play. They needed some clarity, and they needed it now. If the situation did not change then and there, England's World Cup could be over come Saturday afternoon in Nantes.

The management, who were keen to provide the players with authority and to be totally involved in the decision-making process, took it all on board and agreed. Every player was invited to have his say, and almost everyone did. It would not have been the most comfortable hour in Brian Ashton's life, nor for his team of coaches, but given that a common goal was being sought, he

'The simple fact now is that we have to play two cup finals in two weeks and win them both.'

Brian Ashton

was more than happy to listen and react. Different moves were thought up on the training field; players such as Jonny Wilkinson, now back in training, took a firmer control of proceedings out on the pitch, and England began to look like a team who meant business.

Martin Corry revealed a little of what went on behind closed doors inside the Trianon Palace Hotel. When asked if there was a great deal of tension around, his answer was stark. 'Yes,' he replied. 'But it's how we use it. Guys get cranky in training and, to be honest, I think that's a good thing. Now is the time to make sure what we say and what we do marry up.'

Ashton, true to form, was prepared to take the lion's share of the stick meted out by the media. 'We have enough good players to perform better than we have been,' he said. 'I take the ultimate responsibility for what's gone on. I accept the criticism but don't accept we haven't got the players. The simple fact now is that we have to play two cup finals in two weeks and win them both.'

The team to play the first of these two cup finals, against Samoa, had a very different look to the one that lost to South Africa when it was announced on the Tuesday morning. It was without the injured Robinson, of course, but on the positive side, both Wilkinson and Olly Barkley returned, in a backs line that saw every single position behind the scrum changed. Andy Gomarsall was in for Shaun Perry, who failed even to make the bench; Wilkinson came in for Catt, who also found himself out of the twenty-two. Barkley was at inside centre for Farrell, who had been downgraded to a reserve, and Mathew Tait replaced Jamie Noon, who was already back in the north-east of England. In the back three, Paul Sackey came in for Josh Lewsey on the right wing,

'I don't think we will ever eliminate the pain of Friday's defeat'

Martin Corry

Mark Cueto for Sackey on the left wing, and Lewsey would be filling in for Robinson at full back. In the pack, only two changes were made, with George Chuter replacing Mark Regan, who returned to the bench, and Joe Worsley was in for his fellow Wasps back-rower, Tom Rees.

It meant another dramatic change of personnel although, to be fair to head coach Ashton, he was always going to reintroduce Wilkinson and Barkley, while two other changes were forced by injuries to Noon and Robinson. His tournament captain, Phil Vickery, was serving the second of his two-match ban, and Lawrence Dallaglio remained out of the match squad.

The statistics revealed just how much chopping and changing had taken place. In England's three World Cup starting XVs, twenty-four players had been selected. Only four of them had been asked to start all of them. These numbers included three different full backs, three different centre pairings, three different half-back pairings, front and back rows.

Martin Corry retained his position both as blind-side flanker and captain and promised the lessons learnt from that Springbok mauling would be put to good use. 'I don't think we will eliminate the pain of Friday's defeat,' he admitted. 'We're not going to hide or kid ourselves. But we will make sure we use it as a motivational force rather than let it be a demoralising one.'

For Olly Barkley the emotion was sheer relief. After securing the man of the match award for his performance against the United States, a rare light on an otherwise dim afternoon, he missed out on South Africa due to an injured hip he was still receiving treatment for. Despite this, England were confident he would be fit come Saturday. 'I feared the worst,' the Bath player revealed when he was first struck down with the injury. 'I was thinking I might be back for the Tonga match or on an early flight

'We're two desperate teams playing for the honour and the glory of our countries'

Mike Jones

home. I had injections, which weren't pleasant, but they seem to have done the job.'

If Barkley was relieved, however, this was nothing compared to how Wilkinson felt. At long last, he was going to play his first World Cup game since his drop goal did for Australia four years previously. With his track record when it came to injury, it was understandable that when he twisted his ankle in the week before the American game he assumed that – in keeping with his luck post-2003 – would be that.

'The noise I heard when I went down on the ankle in training meant I was prepared for the fact that my World Cup would be over after the briefest of efforts,' Wilkinson said. 'I'd done my ankle before and you forget what it's like. Then it happened and I just lay there and thought of the pain and wondered: "How will I feel if this is it?" In the past I've done my knees and I've been sitting there in the scanning room praying that it's not going to be a bad result. But there has been a one hundred and eighty degree change in my thinking over the past two years which means I don't get too het up any more. I was never going to be running around getting angry or getting my guitar out and smashing it against a tree. I've long learnt to control the controllable and let the rest go. It was nice to get a good break this time and I'm still in the tournament thanks to all the work the medics have done. So, here I am. Hopefully I can make an impact of sorts.'

It would be England's fervent wish, and Samoa's worst nightmare, if this impact were to materialise. The Samoan head coach, Michael Jones, did not expect for one moment an English repeat of their performance against South Africa when they came to face his Polynesians. Jones, the legendary former New Zealand flanker, who earned a winner's medal at the inaugural 1987 World Cup, understood the score. 'We're two desperate teams playing for the honour and the glory of our countries,' he said. 'I don't see England playing like they did against South Africa. They're just as desperate as us.'

That was probably true although, in Mathew Tait, England had a young man raring to go and unfazed by the enormity of the game in which he was about to make his first World Cup start. The twenty-one-year-old had been trying to impose himself on the English national team for two and a half years since his premature introduction to Test match rugby was marred by that infamous dump tackle inflicted upon him by Gavin Henson during a Six Nations defeat in Cardiff in 2005. Tait was making only his fifth start at outside centre for England since that numbing experience, and it was fair to say he was chomping at the bit.

'I'm very impatient,' he admitted. 'I want things in a hurry and I've been frustrated at not having been given the opportunity, as I see it, to do what I know I can do. My game is about handling, running and creating chances and it's up to those who've been picked to put in performances which say "you can't drop me".'

Tait would have been pleased with the vote of confidence from Ashton, not just in his selection, but also by his words. 'Mathew can see things quickly,' Ashton said. 'When he sees them early enough, he has the pace to capitalise.'

Samoa's squad for Nantes offered few surprises. What you saw is what you invariably got with the hard-hitting Samoans. Despite starting with Brian Lima, otherwise known as 'The Chiropractor' for his bone-shaking hits, head coach Jones lamented the fact that, in his view, the game of rugby union was going soft with its inter-pretation of dangerous tackling, and that he was trying to coach something out of his players that came naturally to them.

'We're having to change our style,' he explained. 'We're having to tone things down. This is the essence of who Samoans are. It's part of our DNA. It's the way we were wired up, to tackle hard.

Unfortunately, you can't tackle too hard now. As a coach I've got to train that out of them and that's an inner battle for me. It takes a big dimension out of our game. It's an important part of our psyche. If we aren't capable of doing big, strong, early hits, as we weren't against Tonga [during their 19-15 defeat the weekend before], the opposition get in their stride and think, "Oh, it's not as bad as I thought it would be."'

That defeat to their Pacific neighbours quite clearly hurt Samoa as much as England's loss to South Africa affected the defending world champions. 'We feel we've let down our heritage and our past teams,' Jones explained. 'We own the fact that last week was the worst in Samoan rugby ever. We've been trying to smile while hurting inside. We can't dwell on it, but we've got to live with it for the rest of our lives. But, if it takes losing to Tonga to beat England, we'll go through that pain. To enjoy the mountain tops, you've got to spend time in the valleys. And we've certainly been doing that this week.'

In Melbourne four years ago, Samoa almost caught out the best England team of all time, storming to a 10-0 lead, which included a try by their captain, Semo Sititi, which followed eleven phases and forty passes. It would later be classed as the best try of the whole tournament. Even on the hour, Samoa still led 22-20, only to succumb late on to tries from Iain Balshaw and Phil Vickery. On the back of that, Jones felt one of Samoa's biggest elements, the element of surprise, had been lost.

'We won't be able to sneak up on them like last time,' he admitted. 'They will be a lot more focused. There is a respect for us now which might not have existed before. We know how desperate they are because we stand between them and the quarter-finals. But, for the little part of the world we represent, these are also desperate times. When you lose, as we did last week to Tonga, you get hammered by your own people. We've done a lot of soul-searching, told some home truths and now we have a chance to go from chumps to champs in a week.'

'We won't be able to sneak up on them like last time'

Mike Jones

Brian Ashton saw some immediate similarities. 'Well, we looked at the South Africa game last weekend and thought that was the worst performance by an England team at the World Cup,' he responded. 'So we're in the same boat in that respect. We now have to ensure that last week's hammer blow is not terminal. Every player knows that a win is an absolute must.'

Indeed they did, although Olly Barkley spoke on the eve of the game of how the straight-talking earlier in the week, and the subsequent change in emphasis out on the training field, should pay dividends against the Samoans. 'We've talked at great length about our attack being overly compressed in the last two games,' he explained. 'We're on the same wavelength about what we need to do. If we get it right, everything will click into place with people running into the right areas at the right times. We don't want to get into a bash-crash battle, but if someone wants to take my head off in front of the posts, I'll take the three points.'

The final word was left to Martin Corry who, eight days previously, was left to try and defend the indefensible following the South African trauma. Now the Leicester Tiger was happy to speak of how hard that defeat had hit him, and how determined he was not to live through any repeat. 'We do not want to be associated with two performances like that,' he said. 'I do not want to go through how hard it has hit me because I wouldn't be able to do it justice. It's been a case of, "How can we get better as individuals? How can we get better as a team?" You have to then work that much harder to come up with the answers. We have to use these emotions to bring out our best performance and not allow ourselves to be inhibited by them.'

For all the pressure on them, England knew that they had never lost an international against Samoa before, beating them twice in the World Cup, in 1995 in Durban and then again in Melbourne in 2003, and twice in friendlies, including that 40-3 victory at Twickenham eighteen months ago. Surely they were not about to start losing to them now?

Still, after the tournament they had endured so far, England would have taken any kind of win against Samoa. However, the relative comfort of the 44-22 final score does not paint anything like a true picture, because as the game entered its final quarter it was Samoa, not England, who looked more likely winners until, finally, they ran out of steam.

At first, England seemed to have the game all but wrapped up after they made an instant impression. It took only eighty seconds for England to give their supporters in the 38,000 crowd, packed inside the impressive Stade de la Beaujoire, something to cheer about. When Simon Shaw charged down Eliota Fuimaono-Sapolu's attempted clearance, the ball fell into the path of Joe Worsley just a few metres from the Samoan tryline. The Wasps flanker looked certain to score but the ball would not bounce his way and the chance seemed lost. No matter. From the resulting ruck, and with English numbers poring forward as they recognised an early opportunity, Corry marked his reinstatement as captain by barging over to score a much-needed and very welcome try. Wilkinson converted from close to the corner, and then dropped a goal in the sixth minute.

After the shambles of the South African defeat, and all the tension building up to this must-win Test match, it was the perfect start from an English point of view. Immediately, they appeared to have a better balance to their line-up following all the changes in the team. This was essential if they wanted to avoid becoming the first defending champions to fail to make the quarter-finals.

Samoa, though, were just as desperate to win, knowing that defeat, following their surprise loss to Tonga in their previous game, would end their chances of qualification for the knockout stages as well. Loki Crichton, the Worcester full back, reduced

England's lead with two, well-taken penalties, the second after brothers Henry and Alesana Tuilagi had both burst through England's first line of defence with venom. The calming influence of Wilkinson restored some order with two penalties before his clever grubber kick between the Samoan midfield pairing put Sackey through, and the big Wasps winger made no mistake in touching down the bobbling ball. It had taken just over half an hour for England to produce quick ball, but when they did the result was clinical, and at 23-6 it was looking comfortable.

The Samoans, however, were far from done. They recalled their group game against Clive Woodward's World Cup winners when they led for over an hour against a seemingly better team than the current England outfit and, with six of their backs line plying their trade in the Guinness Premiership, their confidence remained high. In the last few minutes of the first half they came back in spirited fashion. Their efforts were rewarded with two penalties converted by Crichton which reduced England's lead to 11 points at the break.

Crichton was at it again inside the first two minutes of the second half after captain Corry had been penalised for offside. The English advantage had been reduced now to eight points and it might well have been a lot less, too, but for a moment of ill discipline from the Samoans. In the forty-fourth minute high drama took place. The Bristol and Samoan wing, David Lemi, appeared to be speeding down the right wing unopposed. A try looked a certainty but referee Alan Lewis, rightly, called him back and awarded England a penalty after Brian Lima lived up to his 'Chiropractor' nickname by almost decapitating Wilkinson with a swinging right arm. Wilkinson picked himself up to convert the resulting penalty and a likely lead of just one point had instead returned to eleven. Lima, later, would be cited, not for the first time in the Samoan centre's controversial career.

Samoa refused to let the setback knock them out of their stride. When Josh Lewsey's clearance failed to find touch, Lemi and then hooker Mahonri Schwalger chipped on and scrum half Junior Polu beat Mathew Tait in the race for the touchdown. TV match official Bryce Lawrence confirmed what was the best try of the game. England were now rattled, or at least it seemed that way. Wilkinson missed, by his standards, a simple drop goal and an equally easy penalty, while it took Lewsey's last-ditch intervention to thwart a Samoan try on the hour. A lucky bounce of the ball then prevented Alesana Tuilagi from beating his Leicester Tigers team-mate Corry in a chase, and then England had to defend their own line as if their lives depended on it as the Samoans launched wave after wave of attacks.

Although four points behind, Samoa were looking the more likely winners as the game ventured into its final twenty minutes. Even the most stoic of England followers must have feared the worst. This, then, became the pivotal point of England's World Cup campaign. They were on the verge of buckling to a Samoan side that quite clearly smelled blood. Capitulate now and there would be no turning back. England's abysmal tournament would be confirmed. Respond and rally, however, clear their lines, counter-punch and see off the challengers, and England would at least live on for another day. Perhaps more importantly, the fight inside the England players would have finally shown itself. Much later on in the World Cup, the players and team management would look upon the final quarter of this game as the turning point.

On one of their few sorties upfield, England managed to ease into a seven-point lead thanks to another Wilkinson drop goal. In scoring this crucial field goal, Wilkinson became only the third player in the history of international rugby to pass 1,000 points, with only Wales's Neil Jenkins and Italy's Diego Dominguez ahead of him. The Argentine-turned-Italian stood only four points ahead of him now, and he had taken 76 Tests to get there, compared to Wilkinson's 67. Jenkins was a little way off on 1,091 points, amassed in 90 Tests but, injuries permitting, it was only a matter of time before the Englishman became the greatest points scorer of all time. Dominguez passed four figures at the age of 36, while Jenkins achieved the feat a few months before his 30th birthday. Wilkinson, astonishingly, and especially when the lost years and Test matches are considered, made it to 1,000 just a few weeks past his 28th birthday.

He had not finished there, either, against Samoa. The lead became 10 points when England, far from convinced that the game was won, opted for a kick at the posts from a penalty inside their own half. Wilkinson duly obliged, making a 55-metre kick appear absurdly commonplace. At last, as the clock ticked down into the final few minutes, Samoa began visibly to tire. Corry sealed a captain's performance with his second try and Sackey burst over in the corner for his second try of the game as well, to hand England a four-try bonus point. The 44-22 final score undoubtedly flattered the world champions, but the manner in which they answered the serious questions posed by Samoa was encouraging.

'When Samoa hit back to be just 26-22 down, the game could have gone either way,' admitted Brian Ashton. 'We managed to grab it by the neck, though, and believed in our process, and that's what got us through. There were many positives. We got a win, a bonus point, we played with more shape and balance, our defence held strong when it got to 26-22, and we pulled away well at the end. We've taken a step in the right direction but we must improve if we are to make the quarter-finals.'

Martin Corry's main emotion afterwards was relief after the humiliating defeat by South Africa eight days before. 'I'm picked for many things for England, but not necessarily for my try-scoring ability,' the England captain admitted. 'I probably won't get another chance in three years. There have been so many emotions since the South Africa game. We've played below our potential and it was important we showed our hand in this tournament. There's been a lot of frustration but we've had a good

'The Paul Sackey I know is the man who finished off that move in the last minute'

Andy Gomarsall

week's training and it's good to finally see what we've done on the training pitch transfer into the game. We've put in two poor performances, and that was our first decent display in the World Cup. Of course we're pleased, but we're not going to go overboard about it. We're far from satisfied and we've got to back this up next week against Tonga.'

For a man who had just scored two tries, Paul Sackey remained remarkably laid-back afterwards. 'It is the job often for the winger to score the tries so I don't care how the ball gets to me, or how I end up scoring, as long as I get over the line I'm happy,' he said. 'We felt pretty low after last weekend's performance. Emotionally, we were really down. But we went back to the drawing board and got our foundations right. My emotions were high throughout the game. Getting the second try really meant a lot, especially since it killed the game off. Jonny Wilkinson did his little dance in front of me and passed it inside to me and I saw the space. I took the opportunity. It was a proud moment.'

It was a proud moment, too, for his great friend and mentor, Andy Gomarsall, whose influence played a major part in this English victory, and who watched the man he helped nurture when they both played for Bedford score two world-class tries. 'The Paul Sackey I know is the man who finished off that move in the last minute,' said Gomarsall. 'He likes to get the ball one-on-one. He's just a terrific talent.'

Wilkinson ended the day's proceedings with a record and a personal haul of 24 points, consisting of four penalties, two drop goals and three conversions. Missing from the first two World Cup pool games, his impact on his return was immediate and conclusive, yet, typically, he was quick to play down his role, and his latest haul that saw him pass 1,000 points. 'I've been very fortunate to play in a side which has given me so many opportunities,' he said.

'It's a tough environment when you are hanging by a thread and the pressure is really on. You try to keep the tension out of your everyday life but it's difficult. When you start thinking about it on the Tuesday morning, you tell yourself that the game isn't until four o'clock on the Saturday afternoon. You have to find a balance between time looking at computers and videos, talking to other players and trying to relax. It's quite an overload. It tires you out mentally and, while we have ourselves to blame for being in this position, we have to make sure we have a smile on our faces. It's tough when you lose as badly as we did last week, and some people may have expected us to go down today. We've all been in one do-or-die, win-at-all-costs atmosphere and exactly the same rules will apply this week. We earned the right to wake up in a positive spirit to start our preparations for Tonga.'

Having seen off one Polynesian island, England would need to do it all over again six days later in Paris when, this time, they would be facing Tonga in a game in which the winner would qualify for a quarter-final, most probably against Australia in Marseille, while the losers would be heading for home. Tonga had made it quite clear that they would be no pushovers. Having already beaten Samoa and the USA, they pushed a South African team, minus a number of first-teamers, all the way down to the proverbial wire just a couple of hours before England kicked off against Samoa and, if the ball had just bounced kindly for them in a last-minute attack, Tonga would have drawn or even beaten the Springboks before going down 30-25 in Lens. It meant that England, despite getting back on track on the French Atlantic coast in Nantes against Samoa, would not be taking the Tongan threat lightly.

'There's a hell of a lot riding on the Tonga game, that's for sure,' admitted Brian Ashton. 'It's going to be a fight to the death. We've got a six-day turnaround, as have Tonga, and we've got a lot of hard work to be done before then.'

Indeed they had, but at least the England players were smiling again and that, after what the Springboks had done to them, was a very good start.

The unmistakeable silhouette of Jonny Wilkinson, who returned to the England line-up after being injured for the vital match against Samoa. (PA)

Mathew Tait demonstrates that despite the pressure, the England squad's spirits remained high as he shows a clean pair of heels to fitness coach Calvin Morriss. (Getty Images)

Paul Sackey's great touchdown from Jonny Wilkinson's grubber kick helped England to a 23-6 lead just after the half-hour. (Getty Images)

In the second half, Samoa came back at England, and the calm authority of Andy Gomarsall at scrum half (top), coupled with the resolute defence of the England forwards, ensured a strong platform at the end. For many of the players, this period was the turning point of the campaign. (Getty Images)

A Jonny Wilkinson drop goal (above left), taking him past 1,000 points in international rugby, and a late, bulldozing try from skipper Martin Corry saw England home by 44-22. (Getty Images)

Friends and rivals, Matt Stevens and Phil Vickery train ahead of the pool decider against Tonga. (Getty Images)

Tonga perform the 'Sipi Tao' ahead of the biggest game of their lives, at the Parc des Princes. (Getty Images)

'Mad Dog' Lewis Moody takes an accidental knee in the face as Vungakoto Lilo attempts to clear. His commitment set the tone for England's performance. (PA)

(Above) Paul Sackey leaves everyone in his wake in an 80-metre sprint for the line to score England's second try; Mathew Tait (right) touches down after Martin Corry's pass for the third try; Andy Farrell (below) celebrates scoring his first try for England to ensure there was no coming back for Tonga. (Getty Images/PA/Colorsport)

Having qualified for the quarter-finals, the England squad took a well-earned rest at EuroDisney. But it was the comments from the Australian camp that proved the best motivator. (Getty Images)

An early break from Lewis Moody in the quarter-final against Australia helped inspire a stunning performance by the pack. (Getty Images)

Referee Alain Rolland warns the Australian front row, who had no answer to the immense pressure applied by the England line-up of Sheridan, Regan and Vickery. (Action Images)

Simon Shaw gave a towering performance against the Wallabies. (Colorsport)

That man again! Jonny Wilkinson kicks his last and decisive penalty to secure a slender lead. (PA)

The final whistle. Nathan Sharpe and George Gregan look on in despair, while George Chuter is the first to realise England are home 12-10. (Getty Images)

Brian Ashton congratulates his players after England's against-the-odds victory. Suddenly the final was only eighty minutes away. (Colorsport)

Chapter 5: Pool Game
England v Tonga

Friday 28 September at the Parc des Princes, Paris   *Attendance* 45,000

ENGLAND 36		TONGA 20
Lewsey	**15**	Lilo
Sackey	**14**	Tu'ifua
Tait	**13**	Hufanga
Barkley	**12**	Taione
Cueto	**11**	Vaka
Wilkinson	**10**	Hola
Gomarsall	**9**	Tu'ipulotu
Sheridan	**1**	S.Tonga'uiha
Chuter	**2**	Lutui
Stevens	**3**	Pulu
Borthwick	**4**	Vaki
Kay	**5**	Fa'aoso
(Captain) Corry	**6**	T-Pole
Moody	**7**	Latu (Captain)
Easter	**8**	Maka

Replacements

Farrell (for Barkley) 52 mins
Vickery (for Stevens) 57 mins
Dallaglio (for Corry) 64 mins
Hipkiss (for Sackey) 67 mins
Mears (for Chuter) 70 mins
Richards (for Cueto) 72 mins

Filise (for S.Tonga'uiha) 46-50 mins
Filise (for S.Tonga'uiha) 55 mins
H.Tonga'uiha (for Hufanga) 60 mins
Molitika (for Vaki) 61 mins
Taukafa (for Lutui) 65 mins
Afeaki (for Fa'aoso) 67 mins
Havili (for Vaka) 67 mins
Hehea (for Tu'ipulotu) 68 mins

Referee   A.Rolland (Ireland)

England	Tonga
Wilkinson (penalty) 14 mins	Hola (penalty) 10 mins
Sackey (try) 20 mins	Hufanga (try) 17 mins
Wilkinson (drop goal) 32 mins	Hola (conversion) 18 mins
Wilkinson (penalty) 36 mins	Hola (penalty) 55 mins
Sackey (try) 38 mins	T-Pole (try) 80 mins
Tait (try) 57 mins	Hola (conversion) 80 mins
Wilkinson (conversion) 58 mins	
Farrell (try) 66 mins	
Wilkinson (conversion) 67 mins	
Wilkinson (drop goal) 72 mins	

Match statistics

England		Tonga
4	Tries	2
2	Conversions	2
2 (3)	Penalties (taken)	2 (2)
2	Drop goals	0
9	Scrums won	10
0	Scrums lost	0
12	Lineouts won	11
1	Lineouts lost	1
3	Turnovers won	4
82	Tackles made	79
22	Tackles lost	29
5	Line breaks	3
51%	Possession	49%
52%	Territory	48%
10	Errors	13
32	Possession kicked	22
8	Penalties conceded	6
7'52"	Time in oppo 22	3'23"
0	Yellow cards	0
0	Red cards	0

England v Tonga Record

Overall	Played 2	England won 2
World Cup	Played 2	England won 2

The last and indeed only time England played Tonga, in 1999, the score was 101-10 in a World Cup pool game at Twickenham. England were disappointed to concede ten points. Nobody was expecting anything like a repeat this time around, however. Tonga, like fellow Pool A nation Samoa, and indeed like Fiji, who were preparing for a similar winner-takes-all game against Wales, had come a long way in a very short time since then thanks, largely, to the large number of Polynesians now playing club rugby either in the Guinness Premiership or the French league. From whipping boys just eight years before, Tonga were now preparing for the Friday night showdown with England confident that they could pull off what would still amount to a massive shock. As for England, after what they had endured so far in France, a win, and any kind of win, would do.

'I'm not sure you can say that England should always expect to beat Tonga by forty points any more,' insisted England's elite director of rugby, Rob Andrew. 'You have to respect the talent these guys have. Anyone who thinks we can walk into the Parc des Princes on Friday night against Tonga and come away with a comfortable victory has only to look at the video of the Tonga–South Africa game.'

If Andrew was, rightly, playing down the hopes of England fans, Tonga were happy to up the ante. 'I think England will be nervous,' predicted Inoke Afeaki, their experienced lock. 'They should be. We have got more firepower, a good game plan and if they don't turn up and play as best they can, they'll be on the back foot.'

Tonga were probably pleased to see Lawrence Dallaglio, the man

> ## 'I think England will be nervous. They should be'
>
> *Inoke Afeaki*

'It had been a real bastard of a week'

John Wells

who played every single minute of England's World Cup-winning campaign, largely confined to the bench so far in the tournament. The way in which the England forwards coach, John Wells, was talking up Nick Easter, this scenario seemed unlikely to change. The former Leicester boss admitted that England's upsurge in form and fortune was related directly to the crisis meeting that took place following the South African debacle. 'It had been a real bastard of a week,' Wells described, pretty graphically. 'There was no doubt after the South African match that there were issues the players wanted to be dealt with. They were dealt with behind closed doors. A lot of good things came out of it, things which we've been working on. There's no doubt that winning against Samoa has helped. We got a performance of sorts, and now we've got to get one to beat Tonga. This will be a ding-dong battle.'

It appeared that Easter, not Dallaglio, would be the one employed for it. 'Nick has done very well,' Wells continued. 'He brings good ball skills and a good ball-carrying game. It's important for the team that we have guys in the back row who we know we can rely on to make yardage and big tackles.'

The England scrum coach, Graham Rowntree, the former Leicester and England prop, knew that the battle between the two front fives would go a long way to deciding the eventual outcome, and was keen to explain how he saw his men as much more than 'set-piece monsters'. Andrew Sheridan was an example of how much more the front five could do these days. 'Their primary role is to guarantee possession,' Rowntree explained. 'But it was great to see Sheri [Sheridan] carrying the ball twenty metres with four Samoans hanging on to his back. That's a sign that he's not just a set-piece monster.'

He and Wells were faced with a tricky, if happy, dilemma. Captain Phil Vickery's two-match ban for tripping American centre Paul Emerick was over and the Wasps prop was now available for selection again. But, in his absence, Matt Stevens had fared well, especially against the Samoans where his skills in both the tight and loose were aired. 'Matt's game is progressing nicely,' Rowntree added. 'But Phil can bring presence and experience to the team and it will be good to have him available.'

Indeed it would, especially as England saw the battle up front with Tonga to be a greater challenge than it was against Samoa. 'They have a very strong scrum,' Wells analysed. 'They have a line-out that competed very well with South Africa, quite a lot of their players play European rugby in some shape or form, and they're experienced in the darker arts of the scrum and line out. It's going to be a much bigger challenge in the set-piece area than it was against Samoa.'

Vickery was just relieved to be back in contention again, if still aggrieved at the citing commissioner's verdict that his act of tripping had been deliberate. 'The trip deserved a yellow card but I said it wasn't intentional or malicious, and it wasn't. It was completely instinctive. I have absolutely no record at all in the game of violent play. I've no idea why it happened because there was no thought process involved. I just think the authorities wanted to make an example of someone like the England captain early on to make their mark. It wasn't so much the ban that hit me. What I really found hurtful was that the commissioner just didn't believe me, or want to believe me. My character has been questioned.'

Having to train outside the two match squads against South Africa and Samoa was not easy. Having to watch the Springboks run rings around his England team, and then see Samoa push England so close until the last ten minutes was almost unbearable. 'When I got banned I felt I'd let myself, my team-mates and my country down,' Vickery admitted. 'For the next two weeks I felt a bit like a leper. When you're not in a squad in rugby, you're out and, although everyone was very nice and understanding, they also had to get on with planning for the next game without me being a distraction. So I just got on with training from the periphery. If it's possible I felt even worse during and after the South Africa game than those who played in it. I'm sure I wouldn't have made much if any difference, but if we were going to go down that badly, I wanted to be with them out on the pitch. The fact that I got myself suspended made it doubly difficult to go into the changing rooms afterwards and see their faces.'

For a while, when Samoa had reduced England's large lead to just four points, and were bearing down on the English line, Vickery feared the worst as he sat in the stands in Nantes, helpless to do anything but endure. 'It did cross my mind that we could be out of the World Cup and my contribution as captain was to lead us to a poor win over America, and then get banned.'

Luckily, this was not the case, although he was further disappointed the following day when the team management announced the twenty-two-man squad to face Tonga and decided to stick with Stevens. Vickery had now seen his place taken by Stevens, and his captaincy returned, once more, to Martin Corry. He would have to make do with a seat on the substitutes' bench.

'Matt has taken his opportunity well and Phil has not played for a couple of weeks,' explained Brian Ashton. 'We think the best way to ease him back in is to put him on the bench. Matt makes a big impact around the field, and in the circumstances it's the right thing to do. The captaincy issue was secondary to the front row issue. I chose Phil at the start of my tenure and stuck with him all the way through, but I'm perfectly happy with the job Martin did for us last week against Samoa.'

It was a bitter blow to Vickery who admitted it wasn't the news he wanted to hear. 'Well, I'm obviously disappointed,' he said. 'I'd like to be out on the field. But I've been out and Matt's played really well. You have to deal with it. Everyone's been really good and the coaches have given me one hundred per cent support. To be honest, it's the least of my worries. Let's just make sure we win the game and get through to the quarter-finals.'

Ashton was quick to quell any suggestion that keeping Vickery on the bench was further punishment for his misdemeanours. 'I'm a bit more humanitarian than that,' said the head coach. 'I suspect Phil isn't the happiest man at the World Cup, but there's not a lot you can do about it.'

> 'Well, you've got a mountain to climb here but you've got to think you are better than the captain'
>
> *Matt Stevens*

For Matt Stevens the retention of his place came as a surprise. 'I went to bed on Monday night hoping the best but fearing the worst,' he admitted. 'Now I hope to go out and prove the coach's decision right. I would have been quite angry if I had not made it. It's a massive compliment. I'm not blowing his trumpet here, but Phil has been one of the best props of the last five or six years as a modern front row forward. He's someone I look up to a great deal.'

Maybe, but Stevens was determined to keep hold of the jersey. 'I've got to think that way,' he said. 'But in this game you daren't look beyond the next one. We were all disappointed for Vicks when he was suspended but, psychologically, you've got to back yourself. You've got to think: "Well, you've got a mountain to climb here but you've got to think you are better than the captain." I was told by those selecting the team that if I did that I would be picked, no matter what. Fair play to them, they have been as good as their word. I do not want to let them down. Tonga have a good scrummaging pack, so we're definitely not sitting back on any laurels. We expect a lot more of ourselves.'

That was especially the case after the experience of being thrashed by a South African team featuring a lot of former teammates. 'I played with a lot of those guys at school and at provincial level,' Stevens recalled. 'I wanted England to shock the world that night because everyone thought we were going to lose. We felt we let England down but we've taken the responsibility on ourselves to come up with the goods. We haven't done that yet because you couldn't say last week's performance was a superb one, but it was definitely an improvement and you will see a further improvement now.'

For Corry, who retained the England armband despite Vickery's recall to the bench, leading his country in anything other than a caretaker role was something he had never expected. When he led England to defeat to South Africa the previous November at Twickenham, the Test match that resulted in head coach Andy Robinson losing his job, Corry knew his days were numbered.

'I certainly didn't expect to get the captaincy back,' he admitted. 'Brian rang me when he took over to tell me that he wanted Vicks as captain. The old system wasn't working so he had to make changes. I said then that if I'd been in his shoes I would have done exactly the same thing. After every game I question myself, all the more so when we are going through a difficult period. You ask: "What more can I do to make myself a better player?" We put ourselves in a hell of a situation after the South Africa game and didn't hit the heights we wanted against Samoa. We've had one decent performance out of three in the tournament and we are taking Tonga as a very, very dangerous threat.

'Captaincy is not something I strive for. The most important thing for me is that I'm in the starting XV. I thought Vicks would come back for this match, but he's on the bench and will come on at some stage. When he does, he will take his rightful role as captain, but Matt Stevens has done a job and shown this is not an easy team to break into, which is the way it ought to be. It pains me to say this but we have not been deserving of our world title. That's because of how we have played since we won it in 2003. We haven't done the tag of being world champions justice. Hopefully, we are now launching a challenge to the best teams in the world.'

For once England kept the changes in their team selection

'We felt it was totally inappropriate. They will be playing without any green in their hair'

World Cup spokesman

to a minimum. Steve Borthwick replaced Simon Shaw in the second row, while Lewis Moody would be making his first start of the tournament in the back row instead of Joe Worsley. 'Simon has started every game and been on the field for most of them, so it's as much a case of his management as anything,' Ashton explained. 'Joe has picked up a bang on the neck in a couple of games and we are taking him out of the firing line.'

Firing line was a good way of putting it. According to the Tongan captain, Nili Latu, he led 'a team of warriors prepared to die for their country', although by the Thursday 'die' had been replaced by 'dye'. While England were talking about the fear factor of losing this game, the Tongans were busying themselves by dyeing their hair green in support of an Irish on-line bookmaker. The International Rugby Board were far from amused. 'This is the most important match in Tonga's history and the world is watching,' responded a World Cup spokesman. 'We felt it was totally inappropriate. They will be playing without any green in their hair.'

Unperturbed, Latu promised England his Tongans would be giving their all. 'We're going to throw the kitchen sink at them,' he said. 'The losers won't get another chance and we've got the best team we've ever had. It's been a long struggle but we've already made history. To unite our country and stand as one is a major achievement. I hope this game will benefit all the islands because the world will benefit if Samoa, Fiji and ourselves grow. This isn't about a rich team against a poor one. It's about showcasing talent. It's going to be hard, though, because England are beginning to hit their straps.'

The potential for Tonga, if they were to beat England and

provide one of the greatest shocks in World Cup history, could not be under-estimated. 'A whole generation would then grow up with local heroes,' is how the Tongan assistant coach, Ellis Meachen, put it.

The problem with Tongan rugby is that most of their superstars left to play for other countries. When you consider that the tiny Pacific island had produced the former All Black legend Jonah Lomu, as well as the former Wallaby Willie Ofahengaue, who won a World Cup winner's medal in 1991, and Toutai Kefu, who was also part of an Australian World Cup-winning side eight years later, the world of rugby quite clearly owed the Tongans. England looked poised to benefit, too. Rugby league legend Lesley Vainikolo had just switched codes by signing for Gloucester. While England were over in France, Vainikolo marked his Guinness Premiership debut with five tries. He then let it be known that he was eligible to play for England.

Quite a few of the Tongans about to face England were already familiar to British rugby fans. Half of their twenty-two-man squad picked to play against England plied their professional club trade in England, Wales and France, while four more, like the wild-haired No. 8, Finau Maka, played in New Zealand. It was little wonder that Tonga came into the tournament ranked twelfth in the world, their highest-ever position.

One player the English, and especially Rob Andrew, Jonny Wilkinson and Andrew Sheridan knew all about was the big Tongan centre, Epi Taione, formerly of Newcastle and Sale. 'I'd be in the bars in Newcastle until two o'clock in the morning and Jonny Wilkinson would be practising his goal-kicking at around the same time,' Taione, a colourful character, explained. 'I'd say that was the big difference between us. Playing alongside him at Newcastle, he helped me a lot and I'm looking forward to meeting him again. But playing for Tonga means everything to me. This match against England is the biggest in our history. It's the biggest thing Tonga has ever been associated with. It's not going to be

'For me, fear is always a huge part of playing the game'

Phil Vickery

easy, especially now that Jonny is back playing for them. England with Jonny are a totally different team than they are without him. He pulls the strings, which is what you'd expect from one of the biggest names in world rugby. But we are thinking only of winning. Nothing else.'

Back in the England camp the deposed England captain, Phil Vickery, spoke of fear. 'There's no point dressing it up,' he said, in his usually frank manner. 'We lose and we're out. You've got to have that fear there somewhere. The last thing any of us wants is to be part of an England team which doesn't even get out of the pool stages. For me, fear is always a huge part of playing the game. I've always wanted it as motivation whatever game I'm playing in. People are going to have to be edgy and so they should be. These are players who have won big matches in big tournaments. It's up to us to go out and perform. There's no point throwing any blame around. You can have the best coaches in the world but if you don't do the basics as players, you're going to be in trouble. We've got to be better than we have been, otherwise what happened in 2003 could end this weekend.'

At least he was in the match day twenty-two, even though he had not made the starting XV. Dallaglio would be sitting alongside him on the bench, which was a promotion of sorts from the previous two games, but he was still trying to come to terms with his demotion from the starting XV. 'I'll be honest,' he said. 'I didn't expect to come here and not play in that game against the Springboks, but I'm not looking to apportion blame other than to myself. It's very painful watching the team get beaten 36-zip. I shared that pain with everyone else. I've got to try and do something about it and this is the first opportunity I've had to do that. It is exactly what I intend to do.'

The World Cup was not exactly working out as he had

planned, but Dallaglio had no regrets about coming out of international retirement. 'You can't script it all. I've tried to do most of that for much of my career. It's just that whoever wrote the script this time round didn't consult me beforehand. There's no guarantee I will get an opportunity but the priority is not about me, it's about winning the game. Considering what's happened since the last World Cup, it's no huge surprise we are in this position. It's a tricky one when you're not in the match twenty-two. You play a supporting role, which I think I have played well. I stayed calm, tried to work hard and keep a decent attitude until an opportunity came again. If required, I will do whatever I can to make sure we win the game. I enjoy proving the doubters wrong. That's something we intend to do and get a quarter-final against Australia. If we reach our potential we'll be a hard team to beat.'

By the eve of the game England were feeling positive. Their captain, Martin Corry, decided the best way forward would be not to hide behind their previous World Cup experiences, but to stick their chests out and act like the superpower they were supposed to be. 'We expect to win the game,' he said. 'That's taking nothing away from Tonga. They come into this game full of confidence but we are a team that also has momentum in terms of our expectation and ambitions. We're not looking at any negativity. We're positive and we're focusing on us. There is a time for people to talk, and a time for people to shut up and get on with it. That time is now.'

Indeed it was. Come Friday night, inside a packed Parc des Princes brimming with atmosphere, England upped their performance and came out worthy winners but, once again, they faced opponents from the South Pacific who were not prepared to give up their place in the 2007 World Cup without one heck of a fight. England could only breathe easily after an hour of this tumultuous encounter. It was only then that the Sea Eagles of Tonga began to tire, and England could be safe in the knowledge that they were not about to become the worst defending champions in the history of the tournament. Even then, the Tongans had the final say, and few inside the capacity crowd of 45,000 packed into the famous old bowl on the edge of the Bois de Boulogne begrudged them this. They may have shipped a century of points against the English the only other time the two nations met, but they, and Pacific Island rugby as a whole, had moved on and now they could cause any team in the world a scare or two.

Fortified by a quick recital of their favourite prayer from Philippians 4, verse 13 ('I can do all things in Him that strengthens me'), which was chanted in the dressing room, the Tongan players ran out on to the pitch believing that this would be their date with destiny. After the two national anthems, and then Tonga's version of the 'haka', the ritual war dance called the 'Sipi Tao', which took place just a few metres from the England players, the action began and it was Tonga who started much the better as driving rain made the ball slippery and conditions underfoot muddy.

While Hale T-Pole, back from a one-game suspension following his red card against Samoa, started to pile into the English defence, England's players were experiencing early on the sheer brutality of the Tongan game. Lewis Moody, typically, was placing himself in all kinds of danger and it was within the first five minutes that he received a vicious, if accidental, knee in the head as he attempted to charge down a clearance by Vungakoto Lilo. After five minutes' treatment he rose groggily to his feet and continued, living up to his 'Mad Dog' nickname. Later, in the second half, he would come off second best in a collision that saw his head jerked back by the force of an arm smashed into his face by the Tongan captain, Nili Latu. 'I thought God was on my side when the referee let me off with a warning,' Latu would say afterwards, admitting he was fortunate not to be sent off for the tackle. 'I got the tackle wrong and I was glad when I saw Moody get back to his feet.'

Under such early pressure, England conceded the first points of the game when Mark Cueto took a loose clearance into contact and was penalised for not releasing the ball. Tonga's stand off, Pierre Hola, sent a fiercely driven penalty between the posts and, despite its flat trajectory, over the bar to hand his team the lead. It would last only a few minutes before Wilkinson equalised with a penalty, but this seemed to spur Tonga to launch a furious onslaught on the English line.

The English defence held firm for a while but it was clear, as the match clock ticked towards the 20-minute mark, that Tonga were sure to score. Perhaps it was fitting that it was their big inside centre, Epi Taione, who did the damage. Taione first forced his former Falcons team-mate Wilkinson to bounce off his challenge and then fed outside centre Suka Hufanga who dodged past two tackles to slide over the touchline and evade Olly Barkley's last-ditch efforts. Hola converted and England found themselves 10-3 down inside the first eighteen minutes.

Six days earlier England had beaten Samoa thanks to a significant early lead, followed by a storming last quarter after the Samoans had almost drawn level. This time it would be England who would need to find the comeback. There was no luxury of an early lead. Fortunately they possessed a stand off named Jonny Wilkinson, and it was his vision that made their first try of the night. Awarded a penalty on the Tongan 22-metre line towards the left-hand touchline, Wilkinson appeared to be preparing to inform the referee, Ireland's Alain Rolland, that he intended to kick towards the posts. Instead, he looked up, saw Paul Sackey loitering out on the right wing and rapidly sent a long punt from one wing to the other. It was not inch-perfect, by any means, although still a sensational kick. Sackey may have been unmarked, but he still had it all to do. Diving forward to take the ball in mid-air, he acrobatically managed to keep hold of it while, at the same time, throwing his body down to score just an inch or two away from the dead-ball line. It was a marvellously athletic effort by the Wasps winger, and it got England right back into this winner-takes-all game.

Barkley had the chance to give England the lead with a drop

goal but sent the ball wide. Wilkinson, shortly afterwards, made no mistake with a similar chance and suddenly England were in the lead.

Back came Tonga, pressing for a score themselves to reassert their authority. They were looking threatening as they approached the English 22-metre line when Hola's pass out wide to Joseph Vaka was boot-lace low; it evaded his team-mate's clutches and fell into the arms of Sackey. He looked up and all he could see in front of him was an 80-metre sprint to the Tongan line. This was where all those hours of sprint training with athletics coach Margot Wells back in London, paid for out of his own pocket, would count. Picking up the ball and tucking it under his arm he set off, covering the ground in no time, and without a Tongan defender laying a finger on him, he dived over to score his second try, and fourth in the tournament, with three minutes remaining of the first half. Despite Wilkinson missing his second conversion, England returned to their dressing room nine points up having soaked up the pressure for much of the half.

When Hola's penalty fifteen minutes after the half-time interval reduced this advantage to six points, England knew the job was far from complete. Andy Farrell came on for Barkley who, possibly still troubled by his hip, had not shone as brightly as he had against the United States. He could have scored early on if he had received a pass when unmarked on the outside but, from the resulting ruck and some terrific defensive work from man of the match Sackey, England attacked in the opposite direction. When Martin Corry slipped the ball inside to Mathew Tait, the Newcastle Falcon showed his eye for a gap by darting through to score close enough to the posts to make Wilkinson's conversion a formality.

Even then England were not finished, and it was probably just as well. In what seemed like a well-worked training-ground move, Farrell took Wilkinson's short inside pass in full stride to burst his strong frame through the last line of Tongan defence and over to score his first try for England in rugby union. The fact that Farrell

'I'd be lying if I didn't admit to particularly enjoying that try'

Andy Farrell

was mobbed by so many of his team-mates on the pitch not only showed how happy they were to get a fourth try to secure the win, but also how pleased they were for a very popular figure who had earned all his colleagues' respect for what he had achieved in rugby league, and how he had fought back from injuries to stake his place in the England union side.

'I'd be lying if I didn't admit to particularly enjoying that try,' the thirty-two-year-old would comment later. 'Everyone knows the past two years have not gone as planned after I switched codes. There were times while I was injured when I thought seriously about packing it all in, so it was a special moment when I went over for the try.'

For the second week running, England had secured a four-try bonus point. Wilkinson converted and soon after dropped a goal and the game was won. However, there was still time for T-Pole, the pig farmer from Longo-longo, to dive over in the corner for Tonga's second try of the night, confirmed by the TV match official, and converted by Hola.

It made little difference to the final outcome. England had made it into the World Cup quarter-finals where they would play Australia in Marseille, in a repeat of the 2003 final, and Tonga, who had played so very well throughout the tournament, were going home, having made many friends and impressed the world of rugby.

He may not have been one of the bigger names when he left England for France, but Paul Sackey, having been given his chance to prove himself, was grabbing it with both hands. 'All I wanted was to be given the opportunity to make my mark at the highest level,' he explained afterwards. 'I've always believed in myself and all the work with [athletics coach] Margot has made me a better player. It's great to be able to show it on the biggest stage.'

His captain was certainly grateful for Sackey's finishing prowess. 'It's very special to have a finisher of his class in the team,' said Martin Corry. 'If you look at his two tries, they came when we had been under the cosh. His ability to take opportunities is a sign of a team who are growing in confidence. We've had some pretty severe character tests in our time and this one over the last fortnight has been very tough. We had to put our heads down and fight as a team. The adversity has pulled us closer. We've shown great resilience and the coaches have come up with a game-plan which we've bought into.'

A mightily relieved Brian Ashton was quick to praise the same players who seemed to have one foot on the plane home a fortnight before in the French capital. 'I'd like to thank my players publicly,' said the head coach. 'A lot of people thought we were down and out two weeks ago. Now we're in the quarter-finals. We're still not playing to our full potential and we don't know how good we can be, but we're moving slowly along the road towards getting there. We knew there would be times in the game when we were under pressure, but we dealt with it well. Now we know we're going to have to improve to beat Australia.'

It had been a long time coming but, at last, some belated confidence had entered the England mindset. One by one the players appeared into the late Paris night with renewed belief on the back of two victories against South Pacific opposition. Next up were Australia but, suddenly, the mountain did not seem quite so high for the English. 'Of course Australia will be the favourites,' insisted Josh Lewsey. 'We know what they're capable of, but people haven't seen what we're capable of yet in this tournament. Nobody really knows, and that includes us. What we do know is that ever since that South African game we've been really positive. We let ourselves down so badly that night, but we've drawn a line under it as a squad.'

Corry was also a great deal more upbeat than when he led his

'We'll go into the next game as underdogs and it will be a huge occasion, but we're in the hunt'

Phil Vickery

shattered troops off the pitch the last time they played in Paris. 'When you look at where the England team have been in the past four years, and when you read and hear everything that's been said about us during this tournament, the one thing it's all done is brought the players closer together,' he explained. 'We've improved drastically right across the board in the past fortnight, and we'll need to improve drastically again if we are to make the semi-finals. We don't know how good we can be.'

The man he deposed, at least temporarily, enjoyed a second-half run-out from the bench and later promised greater things. 'We've given ourselves a chance,' said Phil Vickery. 'We'll go into the next game as underdogs and it will be a huge occasion, but we're in the hunt.'

To Lawrence Dallaglio the first priority from now on would be defence. 'We need to move up and tackle because the Wallabies are one of the best sides for putting opposition players out of shape and creating space,' he argued. 'We'll have to be at our very best to beat them, but our best is yet to come.'

Wilkinson who, having missed the debacle of the first two games, helped himself to 16 more points against Tonga to add to the 24-point haul he bagged against the Samoans, was another England player who believed that his team's World Cup adventure was not necessarily going to end in the south of France eight days later.

'Beating Tonga and being where we are after what happened against the Springboks is fantastic,' said Wilkinson, who had just eased into second place in the all-time international points list, overtaking Italy's Diego Dominguez with 1,022 points. 'This group of players know how to turn things round. After playing the game for so long it's become inbred in us. What we have achieved is a massive change of emphasis in this World Cup. We've proved that anything is possible and that's what we'll be taking into the quarter-final. People would have given us no chance a fortnight ago. Now the situation has changed a lot.'

He made an interesting admission, too, having just joined his team-mates as they walked around the Parc des Princes waving to their magnificent supporters who, for once, had something to be smiling about. 'I wanted to pay my respects to the English support and to the Tongans,' Wilkinson continued. 'But what I was really thinking about was what we need to do tomorrow as we start preparing for Australia. How should we prepare for what will be the biggest game of our careers for four years? There's no doubt we're going to need some enormous performances, probably from one to fifteen. We'll have to be at the very top of our game. But we'll also have to go out and win it, not sit back and just try to stop Australia beating us. It will mean we're going to have to take risks. We can't just hold out and prevent them from scoring. We're going to have to take the game to them, keep on attacking and not give them any time. I'm convinced the prospect of playing the Wallabies in a World Cup quarter-final will provoke another big improvement from this England team.'

That would be the minimum requirement for an England team that had come back from the dead. In truth, few seriously believed they could venture further in this World Cup. They had finished up second in Pool A behind South Africa, as most predicted they would, but not quite in the manner expected. Australia, in contrast, were looking good, and they had been waiting for four, long years since losing the World Cup final on home soil to the English for this moment.

There were still eight days to count down before the two nations would clash in Marseille, but already, even before the night was over in Paris, English eyes had become fixed on the Wallabies.

Chapter 6: The Quarter-final – England v Australia

Saturday 6 October at the Stade Vélodrome, Marseille   *Attendance* 60,000

ENGLAND 12		AUSTRALIA 10
Robinson	15	Latham
Sackey	14	Ashley-Cooper
Tait	13	Mortlock (Captain)
Catt	12	Giteau
Lewsey	11	Tuqiri
Wilkinson	10	Barnes
Gomarsall	9	Gregan
Sheridan	1	Dunning
Regan	2	Moore
(Captain) Vickery	3	Shepherdson
Shaw	4	Sharpe
Kay	5	Vickerman
Corry	6	Elsom
Moody	7	Smith
Easter	8	Palu

Replacements

Richards (for Gomarsall) 22–8 mins
Chuter (for Regan) 52 mins
Stevens (for Vickery) 59 mins
Flood (for Catt) 64 mins
Worsley (for Moody) 66 mins
Dallaglio (for Easter) 69 mins

McMeniman (for Vickerman) 28–30 mins
Waugh (for Smith) 64 mins
Baxter (for Shepherdson) 64 mins
McMeniman (for Elsom) 64 mins
Mitchell (for Ashley-Cooper) 64 mins
Freier (for Moore) 73 mins
Hoiles (for Palu) 76 mins

Referee   A.Rolland (Ireland)

England	Australia
England	**Australia**
Wilkinson (penalty) 23 mins	Mortlock (penalty) 7 mins
Wilkinson (penalty) 26 mins	Tuqiri (try) 33 mins
Wilkinson (penalty) 52 mins	Mortlock (conversion) 34 mins
Wilkinson (penalty) 60 mins	

Match statistics

England		Australia
England		**Australia**
0	Tries	1
0	Conversions	1
(7) 4	Penalties (taken)	1 (4)
0	Drop goals	0
5	Scrums won	7
0	Scrums lost	2
11	Lineouts won	14
0	Lineouts lost	1
9	Turnovers won	5
76	Tackles made	77
9	Tackles lost	8
1	Line breaks	2
52%	Possession	48%
46%	Territory	54%
7	Errors	9
28	Possession kicked	22
5	Penalties conceded	9
5'27"	Time in oppo 22	5'45"
0	Yellow cards	0
0	Red cards	0

England v Australia Record

Overall	Played 35	England won 14	Australia won 20	Drawn 1
World Cup	Played 5	England won 3	Australia won 2	

Australia had looked extremely impressive on their way to the quarter-finals. They had won all four pool games, including a comfortable victory in Cardiff against a Welsh side that were supposed to ask some serious questions of the Wallabies, but failed to do so, and they also posted sizeable scores against both Japan and Fiji. Only Canada provoked an average display from the Wallabies, but even then a 37-6 final score was pretty comprehensive. The plan, after falling at the final hurdle four years ago, was to try to go one better, and there were many who observed that the Wallabies could knock the hot favourites, New Zealand, out of the tournament, just as they did back in 2003.

Better still, however, the quarter-final in Marseille presented them with the chance to wreak sweet revenge on England, who had had the temerity to become world champions on Australian soil. True, Australia had beaten them since, but not when it really mattered. That was, until now. The players made no bones about what the chance would offer them.

'A lot of the guys are still torn up about it,' admitted Rocky Elsom, who was a certain starter for the Wallabies as flanker. 'England had a great side then, a champion side, but the loss still burns inside many of our players. If you watch the clips you can see how much it gutted them, then having to watch England ham it up on stage. It still hurts a few blokes. You can never beat England enough to repair that loss and, after beating them at home in the recent past, we'd really like to beat them overseas.'

Half backs George Gregan and Stephen Larkham, who were the proud possessors of the longest partnership in Test rugby, admitted that losing that final was the sole

> 'A lot of the guys are still torn up about it'
>
> *Rocky Elsom*

'When you lose a World Cup final it stays with you forever'

Phil Waugh

reason why they had continued playing the game and not retired. 'That was the motivation for me and George,' said Larkham, who would be missing out on the quarter-final after a second knee operation. 'It was just the way we lost the last time.'

Flanker Phil Waugh was the Wallaby who got closest to charging down Jonny Wilkinson's World Cup-winning drop kick back in 2003. 'When you lose a World Cup final it stays with you forever,' he admitted. 'Since losing it in 2003, for those of us involved, it's all been about winning it in 2007 and now England stand in our way. It's going to be a big fight. With Jonny back, they are a much better team. He adds a lot, pretty much enough to make him the backbone of their team. He's still taking his drop goals well, but I also think he's a handy attacking player. Marking him is like marking Dan Carter. You've got to be switched on defensively because, if they're not kicking to the corners, they're stepping inside you and making yards. The best way to counter the threat this week is to control the ball and make Wilkinson do the tackling.'

Another Wilkinson fan was Chris Latham who, arguably with Jason Robinson, was the world's best full back. 'England are far better with him than without him,' he stated. 'He controls the game, steers them round the park and gives their whole team confidence. The revenge thing sells papers. It's about us winning this one. If we do, we are not going to say it compensates for what could have been in 2003. We have to think of England as world champions and show them respect or we'll be setting ourselves up for a downfall.'

Matt Giteau was happy to join the queue, too, when it came to Wilkinson. 'The World Cup is about the best players and it is good he is back playing again,' said Australia's talented, multi-purpose back. 'Once he is in the team, the whole side seems to grow in confidence.'

Interestingly, Lote Tuqiri singled out Jason Robinson as England's biggest threat, assuming he stayed true to his word and passed a fitness test that would make him available to play. 'Jason's their main attacking weapon,' argued the big Fijian winger. 'I don't like to say it, but he's probably the only world-class player they've got. Jonny gives them direction and shape and kicks anything from fifty metres out, but it will be a massive setback for them if Robinson does not play. You can put a wall up against him and he'll still find a way to get through it. We're confident in our defence but, if he's not fit, there'll be a lot less to worry about.'

That comment concerning a lack of world-class players was duly noted by the England team, as was a previous observation made by the Australian Rugby Union's chief executive, John O'Neill, who announced that everybody 'hated' the English. 'If he's not regretting saying that already, then he should be,' remarked Martin Corry. 'All he's done is fired us up even more.'

The England team had celebrated their qualification into the knockout stages by spending the day with their families at EuroDisney. 'We didn't have to queue at all for any of the rides,' reported a slightly over-excited Lewis Moody. Such are the trappings of reaching the quarter-finals. The Monday was spent at their team base in Versailles, before catching the TGV high-speed train down to Marseille. The England players would have been cheered by the sight of Jason Robinson taking part in full training. The Sale Shark was indeed available for selection, subject to a final fitness test. Paul Sackey, Lewis Moody and Mark Cueto also needed to be tested prior to the team announcement.

All the squad would have endorsed Ben Kay's view that just because England had not shone so far, didn't mean they were satisfied with reaching the quarter-final stage. 'We haven't come to this tournament just to make the quarter-finals,' insisted the lock.

'We want to go a lot further. We've got no intention of going home next week.'

Kay, who suffered a dip in form after the 2003 World Cup but had since bounced back into the England starting XV, had forever been reminded about the scoring pass he dropped during the final four years ago which, apart from providing him with some personal glory, might have made it a lot less intense at the end. 'You still think about it from time to time,' he said. 'It would have been a lot simpler if I'd caught it. I remember Will Greenwood saying in the dressing room straight after the match: "Mate, wherever you go, that's going to follow you around for the rest of your life." He wasn't wrong. Fortunately, it didn't have too much bearing on the result and I'd like to point out that Jonny Wilkinson still hasn't paid me any of the millions he's got from the last-minute drop goal.'

Joking apart, Kay was a big fan of the Wallabies. 'Australia have always been probably the brightest team in world rugby, in terms of intelligent thinking and knowledge of the game,' he added. 'You know they'll always do the basics very well and make the right decisions.'

The teams for the quarter-final were announced on the Wednesday. England, true to form, sprung a surprise involving a former rugby league star. It wasn't Jason Robinson, although the fact that he had recovered from that torn hamstring suffered just three weeks previously was nothing short of a miracle. Head coach Brian Ashton had decided to plump for Andy Farrell to start outside Wilkinson in the number twelve jersey after he made a good impression in the second half against Tonga.

Robinson, for one, was delighted to be back in the same England side with his former Wigan and Great Britain captain. 'One of the hardest things for Andy at the moment is taking all the knives out of his back,' was his take, referring to the criticism Farrell had received after the South African mauling back in the pool stages. 'He has played at the top level, he has great experience and he's a valued member of our team. He will not be fazed.'

The last time the pair had teamed up together to face Australia, the opposition came in the guise of the Kangaroos rugby league team in the small matter of a losing Rugby League World Cup final at Wembley twelve years pre-

'One of the hardest things for Andy at the moment is taking all the knives out of his back'

Jason Robinson

viously. Since then Farrell had led his country fourteen times against Australia, and won only three of them. The 44-4 thrashing the Kangaroos dealt Great Britain at Elland Road in 2004 turned out to be Farrell's last league game before he switched codes.

His mate from the glory days of Wigan did not believe there was going to be more Australian success by Saturday afternoon. 'If you don't get your game right, they have the capacity to score points,' Robinson pointed out. 'We have to get it right and take the game to them. You cannot afford to sit back against a team like Australia. We have to be confrontational and equip ourselves with the right game-plan. It's been a rocky road but we've ironed out quite a few things and we're on course. Now we'll leave the talking until Saturday.'

Even to hear Robinson talking about playing in the quarter-final was music to Brian Ashton's ears. Was it a gamble to play him, though? 'I must admit that when the injury first happened I did think that was the last time Jason would play for England,' he said. 'But it's not a gamble at all. He has done everything required of him and he's fine.'

Robinson was one of six changes he made to face Australia, despite England's defeat of Tonga. Josh Lewsey reverted to the wing as a consequence of Robinson's return, with Mark Cueto, slightly injured in any case, losing out. Farrell was in for Olly Barkley. 'Andy has been looking sharper and sharper as the tournament has gone on,' Ashton explained. 'He looks the right selection at number twelve because of his ability to go to the line and offload, his general leadership and game-management.'

Phil Vickery was back in the starting team as well, both as tight-head prop in place of Matt Stevens, and as captain, taking the armband back from Martin Corry. Wasps lock Simon Shaw returned, after a week's rest, in place of Steve Borthwick, with Mark Regan, similarly refreshed, for George Chuter.

As if John O'Neill and Lote Tuqiri's comments had not done enough damage, Alex Evans, one of Australia's senior skills coaches, threw more petrol on to England's fire by publicly predicting a landslide victory for the Wallabies. 'If the Wallabies play rugby they will beat England by thirty points,' he insisted. 'The English backs are poor in defence and if we run their forwards around we'll smash them. Our fitness and ability with the ball is far superior.'

Paul Sackey was still smarting over Tuqiri's comments. The Wasps winger had scored four tries in the last two games against Samoa and Tonga and had really emerged as a player of international quality. 'All the boys are going to prove Tuqiri wrong,' he promised. 'We have world-class players from one to twenty-two. The boys are up for the challenge. I reckon the comment will come up in the team talk on Saturday to boost the boys to play well.'

The return of Robinson had clearly boosted Sackey. He admitted that in his younger days, when he was finding his way into rugby with London Irish, the former rugby league legend was someone he looked up to. Now that he was on tour with the man, he found having Robinson around to be crucial in his development. 'Jason is an amazing talent,' he said. 'Just training with him and being around him has inspired me to do good things. If you are looking for a "go-to man", then he's your man.'

Sackey had a growing army of fans within the squad as well, though. His Wasps team-mate, Josh Lewsey, was one of them. 'Sacks is a pocket of morale off the field,' Lewsey explained. 'He's a bit of a different character. I think he would probably want to play football

'Sheridan has done a lot of damage to a lot of teams'

Guy Shepherdson

all his life. He's a great poacher. Four tries in two games is an impressive statistic in anyone's book.'

Andy Gomarsall, who helped him when they played together at Bedford, was another admirer. 'We need to find positions for him where he can exploit space,' said the scrum half. 'He's a great runner, and even if he's tackled then he has the ability to off-load.'

For all the threat in the back three, however, England were placing much more emphasis on their front three and, when it came to Australia, especially Andrew Sheridan. The Wallabies were mindful of what happened back in November 2005, at Twickenham, when Sheridan caused so much mayhem in the opposition front row that the game was reduced to uncontested scrums after Al Baxter was sent to the sin bin and Matt Dunning was carried off on a stretcher. This time the little-known tight-head, Guy Shepherdson, would be facing the man recognised to be the strongest in international rugby. 'Sheridan has done a lot of damage to a lot of teams,' said Shepherdson. 'It's strange how that game in 2005 keeps getting brought up. I watched it on TV like everyone else but I avoid thinking about it. He's a fairly destructive scrummager and it will be a huge challenge.'

Sheridan, who had played both in the back and second rows of the scrum before Sale turned him into a prop, is a man of few words. Not for him are the sound-bites of some of his more media-savvy colleagues. The 6ft 4in, 19 stone powerhouse preferred to let his play do his talking. November 2005 was, as far as he was concerned, in the past. 'There's no point giving ourselves pats on the back for what happened two years ago,' he reasoned. 'This is about here and now. It's not for us to talk ourselves up. How good we are is for other people to judge. All we can do is go about our business and work hard in training to try to produce a performance when it matters.'

Would the forthcoming quarter-final prove his world-class reputation? 'I just try and play as well as I can,' was Sheridan's philosophy. 'Sometimes it's good enough. Sometimes it's not and then I have to go away and improve. I don't know about a defining moment but it's certainly the biggest game I'll have played in.'

On the Thursday another injury setback hit England and, once again, Andy Farrell. A calf injury sustained in training ruled him out of the quarter-final and that night the England team management convened an emergency selection meeting after Olly Barkley, who was replaced by Farrell in the initial starting line-up, also injured himself. 'Unfortunately, a flying Phil Vickery ran into the side of my leg,' Barkley explained, with his right thigh heavily strapped. 'It looks worse than it is. I sat down on the bench beside the pitch and then five minutes later "Faz" came and sat down beside me. He did his calf while chasing a kick he'd charged down.'

Now a decision needed to be made. Would the management go with Barkley, if fit, to replace Farrell? Would they recall Mike Catt, last seen against South Africa? Maybe Toby Flood, who had not seen any action since flying in to replace Jamie Noon after the Springbok defeat, could fill the void, or Dan Hipkiss?

'I'd expect to be given a heads-up on it,' revealed Jonny Wilkinson. 'It's not an ideal scenario and it's tough on Andy who had brought solidity and consistency. It's crucial we get on each other's wavelength. But since the South Africa defeat, a lot of desire and excitement has come into our game and the guys driving that are the playmakers. So nothing is unfamiliar to any of us. It's been a huge co-effort. That core has been working together all the time.'

England had no such worries up front where they believed the battle would be won and lost. Joining Vickery and Sheridan in the front row was the recalled Mark Regan, clearly in because of his love of scrummaging, his indefatigable spirit and the incessant banter he throws at the opposition. The selection provoked the

'I like nothing better than a good scrum and the Aussies know that'

Mark Regan

Australian head coach, John 'Knuckles' Connolly, to suggest he had raised his concerns with the tournament's referee manager, Paddy O'Brien.

'Regan is a niggler who over-steps the mark a lot of the time and now that we have spoken to O'Brien he is aware of it,' Connolly admitted. 'They have put him there for one reason – to cause a bit of trouble. He's very aggressive and we hope the referee keeps a close eye on him. We want to make sure he behaves himself, that the game is fair and clean as opposed to the other stuff. Picking him shows their intent.'

It was all manna from heaven as far as the Bristolian was concerned. 'I am looking forward immensely to the first scrum of the match and I'm hoping there will be many of them,' Regan responded. 'I like nothing better than a good scrum and the Aussies know that. I love the physical side of the game, especially when I am among friends like Andrew Sheridan, Simon Shaw and Phil Vickery. This will be a massive battle.'

O'Brien confirmed later that no such topic in his conversation with Connolly had taken place. 'No, we spoke about England scrum half Andy Gomarsall interfering round the base, while England raised the subject of Australia's decoy runners,' he said. But this did not stop Australia's replacement lock forward, Hugh McMeniman, from continuing the attack. 'You can expect anything from England,' he said. 'Definitely off-the-ball stuff, or anything if you're lying on the ground, and a bit of a scratch on the eye.' It would be another remark that would be logged by an England team whose motivation was being provided by one ill-informed Australian after another.

By the Friday the English selectors had plumped for Mike Catt to fill the hole left by Farrell's injury. Barkley's questionable thigh was felt to be too much of a risk to take. Both Flood and Hipkiss

'I guess Brian didn't have too much of a choice'

Mike Catt

would be on the bench in a game where six English and five Australian players who started the 2003 World Cup final would again be starting, four years on. Another two, Dallaglio and Waugh, would be on the respective benches.

The selection provided Catt, who had endured a disappointing World Cup, one last chance to make his mark on international rugby. Lose and that would almost certainly be that in his sparkling career, and for a few others as well. But, after making his England debut thirteen years before, Catt had the chance to repeat what he did in the quarter-final stages of the World Cup in 2003, and that was to transform the game in England's favour.

'I guess Brian didn't have too much of a choice,' Catt said, responding to his late call-up. 'He had to pick me. I know this could be my final international so I'll make sure I give it a real go. We all realise how horribly wrong things went against South Africa and I know when I've played a bad international. I admit I didn't perform, as the team didn't that day, except for Jason Robinson. But two days in this game is a long time. Things happen which mean you can go from number four to number one very quickly. Now that we have a much better understanding of how we want to play the game, being outside Wilko will make life a hell of a lot easier.'

Facing Wilkinson, Australia had Berrick Barnes, who suddenly found himself thrust into the Wallaby starting XV in the week of their pool game against Wales, when Larkham's knee injury ruled him out. The twenty-one-year-old Queenslander had been walking around Cardiff city centre shopping on the Friday when he got the call-up. Twenty-four hours later Barnes shone as Australia dealt comfortably with Wales, and now he had the chance to play against his hero. 'After I watched Jonny drop that goal to beat us in the 2003 World Cup final I went out and bought his books and

DVDs,' Barnes admitted. 'Now I'm up against him. It's a case of uncharted waters for me and I'll either sink or swim. It's surreal just being here, a dream from the days of kicking the ball over the plastic posts in the backyard.'

He would have been cheered by his hero's view on him. 'To lead the team as Berrick does at that age is quite incredible,' said Wilkinson. 'That's something I struggled with at his age.'

All week players, and especially Australian players, had been talking about 2003, even young Barnes, who was inspired by the occasion and the man whose drop goal won the day. But that was four years ago and England knew that what happened that night had no relevance to the 2007 quarter-final, a game in which they understood various styles of play would be required to defeat the Wallabies.

'Australia are the smartest team in the world at working out the way an opposition is playing and shutting it down,' insisted Brian Ashton. 'We have to play in more than one way.'

The last word went to captain Phil Vickery on the eve of the game. 'The past doesn't mean anything,' he reminded his players. 'This is all about our team, our day and our performance.'

Indeed it was. Vickery had no real way of knowing it, but the very next afternoon his England team would produce something so special that, suddenly, and quite rightly, all the exploits of the 2003 England team were put to one side. After a campaign that had tested the most ardent believer's patience, England finally came to the party.

They were written off by the rest of rugby, given no chance against the high-flying Australians, and expected by virtually everyone to be returning home on the Sunday morning. But England, incredibly, would wake up still in the World Cup and it would be the Wallabies who would be leaving in despair. Ben Kay, the England lock, had said beforehand in the dressing room

'Let's have a day that we can remember for the rest of our lives'

Ben Kay

something that struck a chord. 'Let's have a day that we can remember for the rest of our lives.' By Saturday evening it had become exactly that.

The English pack proved to be magnificent on the day, the backs sharp in attack and rock-solid in defence, and that man Jonny Wilkinson kicked the four penalties that eventually sent the reigning world champions into the World Cup semi-finals.

It was Wilkinson's drop goal, of course, that put paid to Australia's dream of winning the World Cup four years ago in that tumultuous final in Sydney, and the Wallabies had made it quite clear that this quarter-final was their chance for revenge. But a week in which too many of their countrymen – notably rugby chief executive John O'Neill, coach Alex Evans, winger Lote Tuqiri, head coach John Connolly and reserve lock Hugh McMeniman – had spoken of their opponents in less than flattering terms served only to give England even more motivation to prove all their critics wrong.

Stirling Mortlock, the Australian captain, had a difficult chance to kick a winning penalty two minutes from time from halfway but he shot narrowly wide and, for once, luck was with an England side who, unequivocally, deserved their place in the following Saturday's semi-final in Paris.

The English pack took most of the plaudits for producing a magnificent performance. Although man of the match Andrew Sheridan and lock Simon Shaw stood out, from one to eight, as well as the later replacements, they bossed the Australian pack into submission, particularly in the scrum and the breakdown.

After the game Australia scrum half George Gregan and half-back partner Stephen Larkham, whose knee injury kept him out of the game, announced their retirements from international rugby.

It was a sad way for two legends of the modern game to bow out. For their team-mates it is going to be another long four years of hurt and regret, but for England, and their head coach, Brian Ashton, it was redemption time at the Stade Vélodrome.

Australia had arrived at the knockout stages after a relatively easy ride, and this will have played its part in the final score. England, so disappointing against the United States and South Africa, had been playing knockout rugby ever since, and their must-win victories over Samoa and Tonga prepared them, mentally, for the quarter-final test.

England had promised to take the game to Australia and that is exactly what they did for virtually the whole of the first half, even though they played under a baking autumn sun which, supposedly, favoured the younger Wallabies. Playing their best rugby of the tournament by some distance, they produced a heady cocktail of muscle up front and attacking play from the backs as they never gave the red-hot favourite Wallabies time to settle.

Lewis Moody set out England's stall early on when, having led out the team to mark his fiftieth international cap, he made the game's first meaningful break, but against the run of play Mortlock nudged Australia ahead with a seventh-minute penalty.

For the next twenty minutes or so, however, it was all England. With six changes to the side that saw off Tonga eight days previously, England appeared fresh and invigorated as they produced quick ball and swift interchanges of play between forwards and backs.

In the eighth minute a Mike Catt chip almost put Paul Sackey away in the corner. Then Jason Robinson burst through with one of his trademark darts, showing he was fully recovered from his injury, only to be foiled by last man Gregan. Undeterred, England continued to press. Suddenly it looked like they really meant business in this World Cup, and it was going to take some doing to wrench their world title away from them.

Eventually the pressure told. Australia killed the ball, then Matt

Dunning collapsed the scrum. Two Wilkinson penalties saw him pass Gavin Hastings's World Cup record number of points. The former Scotland captain had reached 227 points, but Wilkinson is on course to break every record going, and there was little doubt this one would be broken before he finished his time in France.

The English had gained a deserved lead as the front five began to exert themselves on their opposite numbers. All the pre-game pessimism in the English supporters' ranks that dominated the 60,000 crowd evaporated. They, like the players, realised that this quarter-final could produce a turn-up.

Then Australia did what all good sides do. They had spent less than five minutes inside the English 22 in the whole of the half, but when Berrick Barnes dummied to put Mortlock through with a clever pass, a try looked certain. The Wallabies captain was felled a metre from the line by the supposedly suspect Mathew Tait in defence, but Barnes was there to feed Tuqiri and, although Josh Lewsey half-tackled the big Fijian, Tuqiri scrambled over. He scored, of course, in the 2003 World Cup final, when he out-jumped Jason Robinson to catch Stephen Larkham's crossfield punt, and this was a very good time to open, somewhat belatedly, his 2007 World Cup account.

Mortlock converted from the touchline and, with Wilkinson missing two penalties in the half, Australia went into half time believing the force was now with them. England's body language, as they sprinted for the tunnel, suggested this was far from over. They may have been down at 10-6, but they definitely did not feel out. The next score would be vital.

It came to England, and again it followed concerted pressure close to the Australian line. Not for the first time the loose-head, Andrew Sheridan, was giving his opposite number, Guy Shepherdson, a torrid time in the scrum, and when an English ruck threatened to end with a score, Gregan was caught offside. Wilkinson popped over the penalty and England were just one point down.

On the hour they turned this one-point deficit into a two-point lead when flanker Rocky Elsom was penalised for being caught offside and preventing Nick Easter from making a break at the base of the scrum a couple of metres from the Australian line. The flanker was lucky not to see a yellow card but his team were punished by Wilkinson's fourth successful penalty of the afternoon.

> 'I was thinking: "Miss, please miss"'
>
> *Jason Robinson*

> 'I was thinking: "Miss the bloody thing"'
>
> *George Chuter*

Now Australia realised, with just a quarter of the match remaining, that they were in trouble. Barely any of their outstanding backs, so effective in the pool stages, had been noticed as England's wrench-like grip tightened. With sixteen minutes left, on came four Wallabies from the bench, while England responded by bringing on Toby Flood for Mike Catt, replacing an injured Moody with Joe Worsley, then Easter with Lawrence Dallaglio. George Chuter and Matt Stevens had already come on for Mark Regan and captain Phil Vickery.

As the seconds ticked away Australia grew increasingly desperate. Wilkinson had a penalty chance from the halfway line which would have probably settled it with only five minutes remaining, but fell wide. Then came Mortlock's chance, after Worsley was penalised in the ruck. 'I was thinking: "Miss, please miss,"' Jason Robinson admitted later. Joe Worsley felt even worse. 'You could say I wanted to make the finale all the more exciting for everyone watching back home,' he said later, with a wry smile. 'But, on second thoughts, it would have been better for me to have stayed out of that ruck. Once he'd missed it I thought: "Thank God for that."'

George Chuter was given a climatic clue a split second before Mortlock's boot connected that the ball would swing England's way. 'I was thinking: "Miss the bloody thing,"' he said. 'Then, as he lined it up, the Mistral started to blow up and I thought: "Someone up there is looking down on us."'

His captain, Phil Vickery, was more confident. 'I knew Stirling wouldn't make it. He's a great player, absolutely world-class, but it was always going to be our day.' The stadium went quiet, the clock read two minutes and sixteen seconds remaining, the Australian captain struck it hard and true at an angle from the left side of the halfway line, and the ball sailed just a couple of feet past. The margin was tiny, but the impact massive. Somehow, and quite amazingly, England had won.

Jonny Wilkinson may have been the man who kicked all of England's 12 points as he raced past Gavin Hastings's total to end the day on 234 World Cup points, but he knew who were the real heroes of the day, hailing the effort of the forwards who provided the backbone of England's epic victory, exemplified by Simon Shaw and man of the match Andrew Sheridan. 'They were absolutely immense,' said Wilkinson. 'Their sheer desire was incredible. We had some big guys getting through a hell of a lot of work and that saved us. They fought fearlessly.' Wilkinson was also keen to shed light on how much had changed in such little time. 'Since the South African match this England side have been very honest with each other,' he explained. 'Not everyone was on the same wavelength. We came out of that and have played better now. We want to build on this. We'll celebrate this victory and the fact that we're playing again.'

The statistics spoke for themselves. The England pack lost no scrums, they conceded no lost lineouts and were responsible for winning nine turnovers. No wonder Australia failed to make much of an impact when they attacked. On nine occasions they ended up losing the ball. It was not surprising that Vickery, back in the England starting XV, cut an emotional figure afterwards.

'I'm struggling to find the right words,' said the tight-head. 'To win the World Cup is a huge thing, but to beat Australia after everything that's gone against us makes it ultra-special. Some very

'I'm living in Sydney and it gives me bragging rights for four more years'

Trevor Woodman

strange things happen in sport and you write people off at your peril. I feel very privileged, not just to captain this team, but also to make a lot of people back home and in the stands here very happy. It is a great relief. There have been a lot of very agitated players in the squad over the past few weeks. Our success in 2003 was down to sheer grumpiness and a refusal to lose.

'I look at our team today and we have so many gifted players, but we also refused to bow out. It wasn't the purest game of rugby but it was fantastic to be part of. We won through belief, doggedness and determination. It's been a tough tournament for all of us. We've been put under huge amounts of pressure. Today was fantastic for all the boys and for the English supporters. We put our bodies in places where it hurts and we reached a level of performance not seen or sustained in the tournament to date. But we've also had a large amount of criticism, some of it justified. The large majority hasn't been and we are a group of very proud Englishmen who are representing our country.'

Vickery also revealed that his 2003 World Cup-winning partner in crime, Trevor Woodman, had been in touch hours before the kick-off. 'Mate, you've got to win,' said the 2003 loose-head, who was forced to retire through a neck injury and now lived Down Under. 'I'm living in Sydney and it gives me bragging rights for four more years.'

Jason Robinson, quite evidently, was joyous in victory, and equally joyous in having played no small part in the result when, just three weeks earlier, his World Cup, courtesy of his hamstring, appeared over. 'Who expected us to win today?' he asked. 'Nobody, except us. Every man and his dog said we couldn't win. I cannot praise our forwards enough. There isn't a man in our dressing room that isn't cut or bruised, but bruises and lumps

'There was lots of abuse from certain Aussie individuals in the press, so it's really good to send them packing'

Mike Catt

never feel so bad when you have won. This team have been under immense pressure, but we knew we could produce a performance like that. We weren't going to take a backward step and I think we surprised a lot of people.'

Head coach Ashton disliked singling out individual players for praise, but even he had to pay homage to his pack. 'To say the forwards' effort was magnificent is an understatement,' he said. 'They won every area of their game. We knew they'd be strong in the scrummage and in the lineout, but it was pleasing to see us winning the breakdown, too. I'm delighted for all the players. We've put a tremendous amount of work in since the South Africa game and have reaped the rewards. We are a team that came together five weeks ago. It's taken us five games to come together today. In the first thirty minutes we played some of the best rugby anyone's played against Australia in recent years. There's never any question about physical courage with these players, that's a given, but we showed the other kind of courage today in the first twenty minutes, playing the way most people expected Australia to perform. It was a more balanced and complete performance than anything we've produced in the tournament.'

Mike Catt revealed afterwards how all the Australian taunting beforehand had fired up the team. 'There was lots of abuse from certain Aussie individuals in the press, so it's really good to send them packing,' said the inside centre. 'That sort of stuff has no place in rugby. I can't understand why people do it because it is always going to come back and smack you in the face. Still, it was nice to stick two fingers up at the Aussies. It's been a massive transformation. In many ways it was an even better performance than the one we gave to win the World Cup in Sydney four years ago, because then we were expected to win and it was just a matter of executing it on the day. Here, nobody gave us any real chance, so it's a massive achievement to have turned the formbook on its head.'

Mark Regan had been singled out before the game for his alleged dirty play and he was more than happy to respond afterwards. 'I love that kind of stuff,' he said. 'If they worry about me, it stops them focusing on the rugby. We were always going to use our scrum as a weapon, but we were frustrated with the way it was being refereed at the start. The Aussies were a bit chirpy in the first five minutes. One of them was shouting off. I couldn't quite hear what he was saying but after the first couple of scrums I turned round and said: "Hang on, our kid, because you've got another seventy-five minutes of this. So chill out."

'I knew we had them when we scored our third penalty to reduce their lead to a point in the second half. They had a scrum which we made a mess of, kicked it hurriedly to touch on their own line, making only a few yards, and then collapsed our maul following a lineout take. It was the key moment in the game. There's been a lot of soul-searching in the England camp. Today we came together like a band of brothers.'

Nick Easter, meanwhile, wanted to thank the media for writing his team off. 'Borrowing a quote from Nick Faldo after he won the Open, I'd like to thank the press from the heart of my bottom. You guys have given us the siege mentality we needed to pull off this win.'

It seemed every English player wanted to have his say. 'Any time you beat the Aussies in any sport it is a great time for a proud Englishman,' added Mathew Tait. 'To do it in the knock-out phase of the World Cup is even sweeter.'

For the first time since the game against the USA, Lawrence Dallaglio had played a part, albeit small, in the proceedings. He could see similarities developing between this squad and the one that became world champions. 'The important thing is that we

'A couple of our players had been in a restaurant on Friday night and had been applauded as they left'

Lawrence Dallaglio

have stuck together as a group,' he explained. 'Everyone has been bagging us, but there are similarities with 2003 because every game was a real test for us in different ways then. We came up with the right answers then and we have the same, battle-hardened mentality now. It was time we rewarded the fans, too. I told the players before the kick-off to think of the fans. A couple of our players had been in a restaurant on Friday night and had been applauded as they left. Well, if they could get that reaction just for eating ...'

For Andy Gomarsall, who dominated the great George Gregan, the World Cup story was getting better and better. 'It wasn't pretty, a bit like my face, and I can't quite believe it, to be honest,' said the scrum half. 'It was sheer grit and bloody-mindedness. The determination was phenomenal. We believed we could do it, plenty believed we couldn't, but the fans were unbelievable. Every time we got a turnover they inspired us to victory. When the last whistle went I just collapsed in total exhaustion. It was just relief and the most emotional feeling of my career.'

Vickery had spoken before the game about the fear factor. Martin Corry endorsed this afterwards. 'If we'd lost we would have been remembered for being thrashed by South Africa,' he said. 'The fear factor played an important part. People thought Australia only had to turn up and that hurt us. We have also become very battle-hardened. Just fighting to emerge from the group did that for us. I'm not sure Australia had that same hard edge as we did. There was a big buzz in the dressing room. We just weren't ready to go home.'

For Australia, another defeat by England was especially galling, having lost to them in the 1995 quarter-finals and again in the

final four years ago. 'We never got momentum, England disman-
tled our breakdown and we lost our composure,' said the Wallabies
head coach, John Connolly, who stood down from his post as a
result of this defeat. 'England's scrum was world-class and I've said
all along that having Wilkinson in their ranks makes them very
dangerous. We hung on, that's probably the best you could say in
the scrum. Vickery's a wonderful prop and we know how good
Sheridan is. At times we got out of jail. At times we were under
pressure and we didn't cope with it.'

This Connolly put down to the lack of pressure experienced by
southern hemisphere rugby. England, in contrast, fielded seven
players who featured in the Heineken Cup final the previous May.
'The southern hemisphere nations play a freer type of rugby
because there is never any danger of a team losing its status whereas, in Europe, where there is more at stake, fewer risks are taken.'

Captain Stirling Mortlock was almost speechless with disappointment, both for his team and for himself after that last-gasp
penalty went a fraction wide. 'It's right to say I'm bitterly disappointed,' he stated. 'A number of my kicks were extremely close. I
should have kicked them and then it would have been a different
game. We have an extremely quiet and dull changing room.
Having said that, a lot of credit must go to England and the way
they attacked the breakdown and upset our rhythm.'

So England would now be at the World Cup for the tournament's duration, either as finalists or playing in the third/fourth
place play-off match the night before at the Parc des Princes in
Paris. But who would be their semi-final opponents?

If the day had not been extraordinary enough, the night would
continue in a similar vein. France played New Zealand in the
Saturday's second quarter-final in, of all places, Cardiff. Having
lost the World Cup opening game against Argentina, they managed to beat an off-colour Ireland to finish group runners-up. The
Pumas, as winners, had a comparatively easy quarter-final draw
against Scotland, which they would go on to win, albeit with

unexpected difficulty. France's prize for finishing second in the group was to take on the tournament favourites, New Zealand, who had swatted everyone aside in their group. The nightmare scenario of the tournament hosts being knocked out of their own World Cup in another country looked odds-on.

But France, being France, had other ideas and launched a stunning second-half comeback to beat New Zealand and send the All Blacks packing yet again. That night down in Marseille the most extraordinary event happened. A huge Anglo-French love-in took place around the Vieux Port area of the city. English rugby supporters were chanting 'Allez Les Bleus', and French fans were responding with 'Come on England'. Both sets were genuinely delighted for each other on a truly wonderful day for the World Cup – unless you were Antipodean – and excited about the prospect of their next game.

The first World Cup semi-final would take place in seven days' time, at the Stade de France in Paris, between France and England. It had been a victory for the much-maligned Northern Hemisphere, and it was fair to say the whole of England and France could not wait to see the next exciting instalment in what had fast become a World Cup script that nobody could have thought up. England's odds on winning the World Cup had been, after that horrific loss to South Africa, as high as 279-1. Even before the quarter-finals the bookmakers were offering 50-1. Not any more. Unbelievably, England were now just eighty minutes away from a second, successive World Cup final. Their odds to win the tournament had been slashed to 14-1. It seemed a fair bet to make, except for one thing. France – the host nation, in their biggest stadium, and after dismissing New Zealand – were waiting for them, and they recalled with graphic detail their semi-final loss to the English back in 2003. Like the Australians, revenge was on the menu for France.

That night in Marseille, however, belonged to England and the players were allowed to enjoy themselves after their sterling

'You've got to know when to hold'em, know when to fold 'em'

Kenny Rogers

endeavours. On the bus ride back to the team hotel Matt Stevens picked up his guitar and treated his team-mates to what was fast becoming England's unofficial team anthem, a song called 'The Gambler' by Kenny Rogers. 'You've got to know when to hold 'em, know when to fold 'em, know when to walk away and know when to run...' sang the team on their journey away from the Stade Vélodrome.

It could have been written for England's 2007 campaign.

Chapter 7: The Semi-final – England v France

Saturday 13 October at the Stade de France, Paris   *Attendance* 80,000

ENGLAND 14		FRANCE 9
Robinson	15	Traille
Sackey	14	Clerc
Tait	13	Marty
Catt	12	Jauzion
Lewsey	11	Heymans
Wilkinson	10	Beauxis
Gomarsall	9	Elissalde
Sheridan	1	Milloud
Regan	2	Ibanez (Captain)
(Captain) Vickery	3	De Villiers
Shaw	4	Pelous
Kay	5	Thion
Corry	6	Betsen
Moody	7	Dusautoir
Easter	8	Bonnaire

Replacements

Hipkiss (for Lewsey) 39 mins	Chabal (for Pelous) 25 mins
Worsley (for Moody) 54 mins	Michalak (for Beauxis) 51 mins
Stevens (for Vickery) 56 mins	Szarzewski (for Ibanez) 51 mins
Chuter (for Regan) 65 mins	Dominici (for Heymans) 61 mins
Flood (for Catt) 69 mins	Poux (for De Villiers) 66 mins
Richards (for Gomarsall) 70 mins	Harinordoquy (for Betsen) 67 mins
Dallaglio (for Easter) 70 mins	

Referee   J.Kaplan (South Africa)

Scorers

England	France
Lewsey (try) 2 mins	Beauxis (penalty) 8 mins
Wilkinson (penalty) 47 mins	Beauxis (penalty) 18 mins
Wilkinson (penalty) 75 mins	Beauxis (penalty) 44 mins
Wilkinson (drop goal) 78 mins	

Match statistics

England		France
1	Tries	0
0	Conversions	0
(3) 2	Penalties	3 (3)
1	Drop goals	0
6	Scrums won	7
0	Scrums lost	0
12	Lineouts won	19
2	Lineouts lost	4
6	Turnovers won	3
86	Tackles made	81
11	Tackles missed	11
1	Line breaks	0
47%	Possession	53%
45%	Territory	55%
2'54"	Time in oppo 22	4'27"
7	Errors	9
40	Possession kicked	47
9	Penalties conceded	6
0	Yellow cards	0
0	Red cards	0

England v France Record

Overall	Played 90	England won 48	France won 35	Drawn 7
World Cup	Played 4	England won 3	France won 1	

Mark Regan and Andrew Sheridan practise their scrummaging ahead of the semi-final against France, who were expected to give them a much sterner test than the Wallabies. (Getty Images)

Out of adversity, this England team had pulled together and were now ready to take on anyone. (Eddie Keogh/Reuters/Corbis)

After seventy-five seconds Josh Lewsey pounces while Damien Traille hesitates, to set England on the way in their semi-final against France. (Getty Images)

With England trailing 9-5 early in the second half, and France dominating possession, Mathew Tait's run almost brought a try in the corner and restored hope. (Colorsport)

Into the last quarter: Joe Worsley's vital tap-tackle (top) stopped a certain try for Vincent Clerc that would surely have put France out of reach; Dimitri Szarzewski high tackles Jason Robinson (above), and the resulting penalty saw England take the lead with only five minutes left on the clock; even so, the rampaging Sébastien Chabal (left) could have scored a late try, but Paul Sackey and Toby Flood came to the rescue. (PA/Getty Images/Action Images)

Two minutes remain and Jonny Wilkinson drops a goal to secure a 14-9 lead for England – a place in the final was almost there. (Getty Images)

The referee blows the final whistle and (left to right) Ben Kay, George Chuter, Andrew Sheridan, Mathew Tait and Martin Corry begin the celebrations. (Colorsport)

Nick Easter in training for the biggest game of his life – the World Cup final against South Africa. After all that had gone before, the entire squad were ready for anything. (PA)

The England team sing the National Anthem, backed by massive support in the stands, as they get ready to take on South Africa and hope to complete one of the greatest sporting comebacks of all time. (Getty Images)

With the score at 6-3, Martin Corry's tackle on John Smit just short of the tryline was crucial to keep England in the game in the first half. (Colorsport)

Early in the second half, and England had their best moments. First, Mathew Tait (above) made a brilliant 45-metre break that almost brought him a try. Then, after quick ball, Mark Cueto (left) went in at the corner, only for his foot to touch the line just before he grounded the ball. (Getty Images)

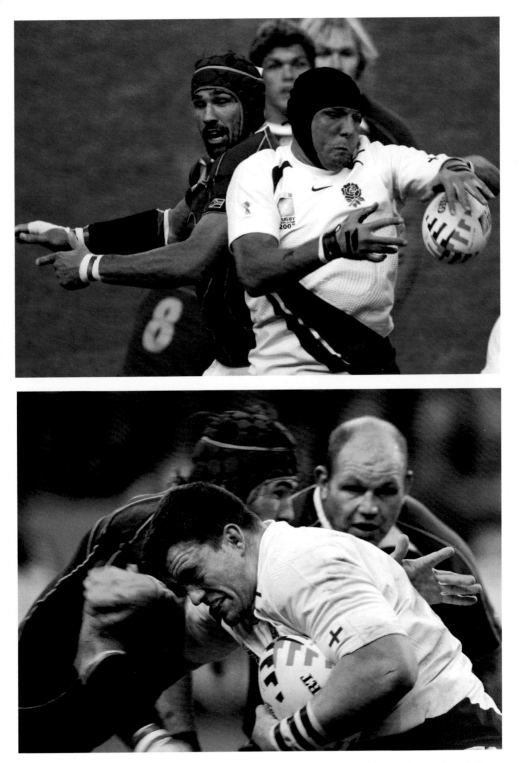

Ben Kay had a towering World Cup for England and was the only player to be on the pitch for every minute of the campaign; Andrew Sheridan established himself as one of the world's greatest props during the tournament, a worthy adversary for the watching veteran Os du Randt, who would soon pick up his second World Cup medal. (Getty Images)

Lawrence Dallaglio consoles Jason Robinson at the end of the match after losing to South Africa 15-6. For both men, there was to be no dream repeat of 2003. (Colorpsort)

Phil Vickery's World Cup had started disastrously, but as the weeks had passed, and England's fortunes had turned for the better, the England captain's quiet but assured influence on the squad was becoming more and more obvious. You might have thought he would be nervous about the big match when he set off from Marseille on the Monday morning to catch the TGV train back to the new team hotel in Paris. But think again. Times like these should be enjoyed, he reasoned. This, after all, was why rugby players did what they did.

'In this game, win or lose, you've got to enjoy the moment because if you don't, you become a dreary old man,' was Vickery's take on life at the World Cup. 'We're going to the semis, where we're going to be underdogs again, but let's go out, look forward to it and enjoy it. Instead of being weary and down about things, let's savour it and play the game with a smile on our faces.'

The thought of Trevor Woodman's latest text message, and the image of his former England front-row colleague making the most of England's victory Down Under, made him smile. 'Looked like you were near to tears on telly mate,' it read. 'You've got to stop 'cos it's making me reach for the Kleenex.'

Vickery and Woodman played together in that epic final in 2003, but the present England captain had made a point not to watch a re-run of that game since. 'I'll look at it one day, but I've always thought that when you start looking back at things like that, it signals that it's the end for you. I

> 'In this game, win or lose, you've got to enjoy the moment because if you don't, you become a dreary old man'
>
> *Phil Vickery*

don't want it to be over just yet. I want to go on and still achieve.'

No wonder Vickery had a smile on his face. Two years previously, he could not even lift his baby daughter, such was the pain from his back. Around the same time, he was on four daily doses of morphine and being told by surgeons that, at best, it was fifty-fifty whether he'd ever play again. It made the criticisms of him getting himself banned after the American game, and the suggestions that he was not missed as captain when Martin Corry took over, or as tight-head when Matt Stevens stood in, seem light in comparison. 'People have tried to make a big thing of the captaincy and me and Martin, but there's no animosity between us. You won't find a better bloke than Martin Corry. Matty Stevens has done fantastically well and will go on to be one of the best props in world rugby, but I'm not lying down yet.'

He and his wife, Kate, were afforded mass applause when they looked for somewhere to Sunday lunch in Marseille. Lawrence Dallaglio had been high-fiving fans in the small hours in the streets of the Vieux Port after the team meal of ribs and chips while, twelve hours later, he, Paul Sackey and Simon Shaw went forty minutes out of town to eat. 'We tried to get a taxi back to Marseille afterwards,' Sackey revealed. 'But we forgot the South Africa v Fiji game was on and there weren't any. A bloke offered us a lift in his boat. It took us four hours.'

The three at least found the easy way to get back to Paris, along with the rest of the England squad, as the TGV sped northbound towards the French capital. The forwards coach, John Wells, was keen to highlight Shaw's immense contribution to this World Cup campaign. 'We've never had a natural replacement for Jonno [Martin Johnson] who had the skills he had,' said Wells. 'Simon's ability to play the ball out of the tackle, his support play and attacking skills meant that he gave us a tremendous performance. He wanted to show us he could deliver consistent performances and we've backed him. The issues with Simon have been to do with that, and fitness. He and his team-mates were grumpy and horrible last week and we won, so I want us to be grumpy and horrible this week as well.'

Graham Rowntree, England's scrummaging coach, was already eyeing up the French pack who, unlike Australia, were likely to present a stiff challenge up front. 'If you're going to beat any French side, you've got to be able to take the energy from them in the scrum because they build from there. They've got a wily old pack and one I've got a lot of respect for. It's going to be a big challenge and we've got to make sure our game is up there.'

In truth, Rowntree had few doubts that the forwards would not be. He hailed Vickery's performance as a prop, rather than as captain, against the Wallabies. 'That was one of Phil's best games at any level for a long time,' he added. 'His work-rate, his tackles and his scrummaging were all right up there. He led from the front.'

He felt the same about Andrew Sheridan, too, although he also posed a challenge for the big Sale Shark. 'Sheri has played well for England before, but not to that level,' Rowntree said. 'He's an incredibly strong bloke and has always had that physical durability, but he's also very conscientious and does a lot of analysis of opponents. His application and work-rate are second to none. But the mark of a great player is the ability to do it, week in, week out. Let's see if he can do it again. If he can, and again the following week, then he's world class.'

Although Jonny Wilkinson had kicked all of England's 12 points in beating Australia, to add to the 40 points he had scored since recovering from injury against Samoa and Tonga, his radar, by his very high standards, had been slightly off-key. It was proving to be a bit of a mystery. Wilkinson's success ratio had dropped by 20 per cent. Checks carried out privately by England's technical staff discovered that the Gilbert balls he had used had been over-inflated. The balls, according to instructions from their manufacturers, were supposed to be pumped to the 'optimum' level of 9.5lb per square inch. England, however, claimed that for their opening game, the disappointing display against the USA, 10.5lb showed on the pressure gauge, and that they believed subsequent balls had been even more pressurised. A ball at the wrong pressure changes its characteristics, both when struck and in flight, and at this level it could, and indeed did, make a difference. Wilkinson, for example, had the greatest of sympathy for Stirling Mortlock, after the Australian captain missed that late quarter-final penalty that would have beaten England if successful. 'It was a damned fine kick,' Wilkinson insisted. 'With the balls flying the way they are, he has real sympathy from me. As a kicker here you are not completely accountable. Sometimes it's like you are almost hitting and hoping, and kickers just never do that.' The upshot of it all was that the six balls earmarked for the Saturday night's semi-final would be pumped up correctly, and that Wilkinson would be allowed to practise with all of them in good time beforehand.

While Jonny had one or two problems with his kicking, his half-back partner, Andy Gomarsall, was just about the happiest man in Paris, and it was not surprising given his remarkable story. If England's comeback had been far-fetched, this was nothing compared to the scrum half who arrived in France very much as the third-choice number nine, but had impressed so much, especially against George Gregan in the quarter-final, that he was now the first choice. That, though, was the least of it. Four years ago, at the 2003 World Cup final, Gomarsall had been one of the bit-part players, out of the match-day twenty-two, and he made himself a private promise that he would be starting in the 2007 World Cup final. It was, to say the least, a big call to make for the man who had spent much of his career in the shadows of Matt Dawson and Kyran Bracken.

It seemed even bigger when, just fourteen months before the 2007 World Cup, Gomarsall was playing for a pub team, the White Hart Marauders from Camberley, in Surrey, having been sacked by Worcester. Disillusioned, the thirty-three-year-old almost gave the game up. 'I was so angry and so low that I could quite easily have given it all up,' Gomarsall confessed. 'There were no offers for me

'Saturday night is going to be pretty damned special'

Andy Gomarsall

but playing in that pub tournament restored my faith in the game. I absolutely loved it.'

Harlequins, finding themselves short of a scrum half, got wind of Gomarsall, signed him up and the man who had rediscovered his love of rugby shone to the extent that he got the nod from Brian Ashton when the World Cup squad was named. 'I'm still pinching myself,' he admitted. 'To say it's been like a massive roller-coaster ride is an understatement. I'd be lying if I said I never doubted that I would get here, not when things happen to you in your professional career and you find yourself on the scrapheap. That does make you wonder, but I had unfinished business with England and a burning desire to finish it. I made myself a promise on the night we won the World Cup in 2003 that I would be the starting number nine for the next one. For me, that was a huge driving force. Now I'm revelling in the opportunity I've been given and loving every minute. Saturday night is going to be pretty damned special.'

Wednesday was pretty special, too, for Gomarsall, and fourteen of his team-mates. That was the day when Brian Ashton named his World Cup semi-final twenty-two. Gomarsall, to nobody's surprise, was in the starting XV, with Peter Richards on the bench as the reserve scrum half. The selection of Jason Robinson meant that the man who had miraculously recovered from a hamstring injury to play his part in the epic quarter-final win, would now be given a chance to run out on to the Stade de France pitch in front of an England team who would be keeping their distance to honour Robinson's fiftieth cap. Even with the man's unshakable faith, this story had him so taken aback that he at once dedicated his half-century to his wife, Amanda, and his five children. 'My big thanks go to my wife,' explained the thirty-three-year-old. 'It's not easy when your husband's away. It causes a lot of disruption in the household and I feel blessed that I've been able to do what I have. To me, it's no coincidence that things have worked out the way that they have. The Lord has taken me from one amazing thing to another. I have been truly blessed.'

Someone was clearly looking after him when his hamstring went against South Africa and his World Cup looked to be over. 'I did have a lot of people praying for me when I pulled my hamstring. Normally, they take a lot longer to recover from than it took me. To be ready now for my fiftieth cap is something very special.'

It would never have happened if Robinson, after Brian Ashton approached him the previous December, had not decided to perform a U-turn and come out of international retirement. 'This all started off when my wife had a vision that I'd be going back to play for England and she wouldn't be coming with me,' he explained. 'We couldn't understand it at the time because, everywhere I go, Amanda comes with me. Then we found out later that she was pregnant. God has certainly made a lot of things happen. The plan at that time was for me just to do one more season at Sale and that would have been it. Suddenly, all that changed. Certain things happen for a reason. The way it had been going with England, everyone was desperate.'

The biggest names in the England squad were keen to praise 'Billy Whizz' on the eve of his fiftieth cap. 'He's unique, a really inspirational figure,' said Mike Catt. 'He's just amazing – a model professional, a good leader, a very influential player and an awesome bloke. That's why we need to play a game that suits his strengths. Jason has two big games left in him, so let's hope we can make them special and give him the swansong he deserves.'

Phil Vickery, even though he called Robinson 'Stumpy', was another fan. 'I used to watch him play for Wigan and Great Britain,' he recalled. 'People doubted him when he came across from league, but the memory I have of him which will live with me forever was when he scored that fantastic try for the Lions against

> ## 'It's another example of the rotten luck Andy has had with England'
>
> *Brian Ashton*

the Aussies at the Gabba in 2001.'

Ashton has always been a rugby league fan and, from childhood days, watched Wigan play. 'I'd been watching Jason in a phenomenal team since he was sixteen,' said the head coach. 'I was delighted to have got him out of retirement and that we have scrambled through to get him his fiftieth cap.'

Robinson and Gomarsall would be part of the same team that saw off the Wallabies. No England head coach had named an unchanged side for two years and for twenty-seven Tests which had conjured up 184 alterations. It meant that Toby Flood retained his place on the bench as the reserve kicker, and Andy Farrell, recovered from the calf strain injury that forced him out of the quarter-final, missed out. 'It's another example of the rotten luck Andy has had with England,' said Ashton. 'But Toby came into a high-pressure match and handled himself exceptionally well.'

France, too, were able to select the same quarter-final twenty-two who beat New Zealand. Despite England's upsurge, the French, who had last lost on home soil to England in 2000, were firm favourites. Only five players remained from that result: Vickery, Wilkinson, Catt and Shaw for England, plus France's Fabien Pelous. The last time they met in the World Cup, however, England won 24-7 in the 2003 semi-final in Sydney, with Wilkinson scoring all of his team's points with five penalties and three drop goals.

Nick Easter was back home in England watching those events unfold on TV. He was little known in the game until only recently, when his surge of form pushed him all the way to the World Cup. 'It's moved fast for me,' he admitted. 'At the moment I don't have the time to think about how quickly things have moved. The win over Australia seems to have buoyed up the whole nation and we're now out to defend our trophy.' Dean

Richards, the legendary former No. 8 for Leicester and England, has been Easter's mentor at Harlequins, where Richards is director of rugby. Lewis Moody, once Richards' team-mate, saw similarities between the two men. 'I hadn't seen much of Nick before, which is a pity because he has been a great find,' said the Leicester flanker. 'He's a big, strong lad, very much in the style of Dean. He stays on his feet and his handling is exceptional for such a big guy. He's got better hands than Dean and is far more athletic. Nick has played out of his skin in this tournament.'

On the Thursday, Wilkinson got to practise with all six match balls and, after a two-hour session, declared himself 'relatively happy' with his workout. 'The session gave me an ideal opportunity to use every one of the match balls and gain a better understanding of them,' he explained. The whole of England was hoping he would repeat his 24-point feat of four years ago, when England ended French dreams at the semi-final stage. 'It's tough to make comparisons between this World Cup and the last one because life was very different four years ago. What has changed is my outlook, because of all that time when I hardly played any rugby at all. I spent a lot of it looking for answers to questions I didn't really need to ask. Would I get back to where I'd been? What was I like as a player? Did I still believe in myself? That took a lot of energy and then the 2005 Lions tour didn't go that well. I've been through the mill so many times that it has made me sit back and treat each occasion for what it is. Sitting in the dressing room before the Australia game last week, I thought how great it was to be there after all that's gone on. I'd never been so nervous in my life. Now it's a case of giving everything to the cause and everything to this game so that it will stick in the mind forever.'

That was what captain Vickery had in mind when he made a final address the night before the semi-final. 'We've got what it takes to beat France,' he insisted. 'But it's going to require every player sacrificing body and soul for the cause. Without that, all the work we've done will be futile. We will have to find a level of

'We don't want to be remembered as a losing semi-finalist'

Phil Vickery

passion we have not found before. People will have to find performances they never thought they had in them. To beat a huge, powerful French side will require physicality, bravery and guts galore. That's how tough this is going to be, but we have the men to do the job and not just those who have been lucky enough to experience a World Cup semi-final before. Every man will have to stand up and be counted because we've got no intention of letting it slip now that we've got this far.

'We don't want to be remembered as a losing semi-finalist. We don't want to be patted on the back at home and told: "Never mind, old boy, you nearly made it." We want to go home as a team who will be remembered for achieving something special. There are absolute heroes in this team. In years to come, we will look back on games such as this one. I'll be here to be shot at if it all goes wrong, but the players in this England twenty-two make me very proud to be playing alongside them. We have the players with the skills and the mental toughness to get the job done. To lose this weekend would make last week's win almost worthless. We know we'll have to perform better than last week, otherwise we will be beaten, and beaten convincingly.'

The semi-final would not go down as one of the great, free-flowing epics of modern times. They rarely do. Semi-finals are universally recognised to be the worst round to fall at in any cup competition. There simply is too much at stake to take risks and make errors. But for sheer drama, tension and denouement, it took some beating. Once again, despite almost every prediction going, England beat France thanks ultimately to a late, late drop goal from Jonny Wilkinson that killed off the World Cup hosts and booked an unlikely place in the following Saturday's World Cup final.

Wilkinson's seventy-fifth-minute penalty had given England a 11-9 lead, but it was the drop goal two minutes from time, from a man who knows when to make his mark, so often in the most incredible of circumstances, which effectively settled this intense encounter. Now the world champions stood just eighty minutes away from becoming the first team ever to win back-to-back world titles.

All this took place on the very same pitch at the Stade de France where, four weeks previously, they went down 36-0 to South Africa in the pool stages. Four weeks on, and England did what teams are not supposed to do in international rugby: defeat France in the French capital when the tournament hosts, seeking to be world champions for the first time, stood one game away from the final. Now anything was possible for a group of players universally written off both before and during this tournament. You could forget about 2003 with Martin Johnson and Clive Woodward, magnificent though it was. If England could close the deal against either South Africa or Argentina, the feat would prove to be far greater than even that of four years ago. At the end, all France could do was watch and, in the case of the old warhorse Sebastian Chabal, cry as England performed the victory lap. Nobody could quite believe just what had taken place.

The early plan for England, once Jason Robinson ran out alone on to the pitch in recognition of him winning his fiftieth inter-national cap, was to quieten the partisan French crowd. Despite the many thousands of white-jerseyed English supporters who had crossed or gone under the Channel to get to the northern Paris suburb of Saint Denis, they were always going to be outnumbered.

Not even the most optimistic of them would have expected the manner in which they achieved their goal. Andy Gomarsall sent his left-footed kick from halfway towards the French line, and the centre-turned-full-back Damien Traille waited as the ball bobbled and bounced. In the corner of his eye he would have seen Josh Lewsey sprinting down the wing. When the ball suddenly sat up, it was the winger who pounced, snatching it out of Traille's hands and ploughing through his man to score in the corner. The clock read one minute and fifteen seconds. Wilkinson missed the conversion from wide out, but England were away.

France responded with a flurry of attacking rugby that led, after some stout English defending, to an eighth-minute penalty converted by Lionel Beauxis after Nick Easter had strayed offside. Despite their appalling start, it was France who played much of the first half with confidence, and it was England who were required to tackle frantically. A second Beauxis penalty, from just inside the England half, after Andrew Sheridan was penalised for not taking the bind at a scrum, nudged France ahead in the eighteenth minute and, suddenly, with the predominantly French crowd getting behind their team, Les Bleus were looking like justifiable favourites.

The good news for England was that the former French captain, and the man with more caps to his name than any other French player in history, Fabien Pelous, limped off in the twenty-fifth minute. The bad news, however, was that the man who replaced him was the French national hero, Sébastien Chabal, who was well-known to his fellow Sale Sharks, Jason Robinson and Sheridan.

By the half-hour, France had enjoyed 63 per cent of the territory and Wilkinson, despite that intensive two-hour kicking practice on the Thursday with all six match balls, had also failed with a drop goal attempt and a penalty from just inside his own half. England's pack were not enjoying anything like the supremacy they had the previous week at Australia's expense, and the joy of the first minute began to seem like a long time ago. When Lewsey appeared to damage a hamstring in the last minute of the first half, the inexperienced Dan Hipkiss replaced him, which forced Mathew Tait to move out to the wing, and so the omens did not appear good. Still, as England ran with purpose back to their dressing room at half time, they were just 6-5 behind.

The French lead became four points four minutes after the interval when Easter was harshly judged to have come in from the side of a ruck, and Beauxis slotted home his third penalty of the night. England responded with urgency and started to play more. A turnover enforced by Lewis Moody nearly resulted in a try in the corner for Tait and, with the French already penalised, Wilkinson sent the resulting penalty between the posts from an acute angle to reduce the arrears back to a single point. There was a story within this story, however. As he lined up to kick the penalty, Wilkinson noticed that the ball did not carry the designated markings of the six official match balls. These six were the balls Wilkinson had been studiously practising with in the days leading up to this semi-final. He was not about to kick a ball he had not kicked before. Revealing a remarkable presence of mind, considering it was in the middle of a World Cup semi-final, he asked for a new ball, which he then coolly slotted home.

'It also happened in Marseille last week,' Rob Andrew, the RFU's elite rugby director and Wilkinson's mentor, revealed later. 'He didn't notice and he missed. This week Jonny was pretty vigilant about it. You've got to get these things right. Four years ago he probably would have let all that get to him. But he's more relaxed these days, so he dusted himself down and got on with it.'

The French made a double substitution in the fifty-first minute. Off went captain Raphaël Ibanez and also Beauxis, and on came the dynamic reserve hooker Dimitri Szarzewski and the mercurial Frédéric Michalak, whose glorious pass the previous week had set up France's winning try against New Zealand. England replied by sending on Joe Worsley for Moody and then replacing captain Phil Vickery with Matt Stevens. Neither side was to know it at the time, but their substitutes would play a massive role in the eventual outcome.

As the game lurched towards the hour-mark the earlier, freeflowing nature of the game gave way to a more attritional battle as both teams became edgy. France appeared the more likely winners

'I knew how fast Clerc is, but I just got a bit of his leg'

Joe Worsley

but, with the clock ticking down and England still just one point behind, the game's finale promised a wealth of possibilities.

The semi-final reached the hour-mark when a firmly driven, right-footed Wilkinson drop goal attempt smacked against the left-hand post. It is with such margins that semi-finals can be won and lost, and when, moments later, Jason Robinson marked his fiftieth cap with a trademark, jinking 30-metre run only to be brought down close to the French line, there were many who wondered whether England's luck had run out.

It looked all over for England when Julien Bonnaire expertly palmed Yannick Jauzion's crossfield punt back into the hands of Vincent Clerc and the French winger charged towards the English line. With nothing but daylight between him and the line, a try under the posts and a simple conversion to follow, which would surely have won the game for France, looked a certainty. Instead, Joe Worsley dived full length and, with an outstretched hand, just managed to clip Clerc's heels and bring him crashing down. Although Chabal collected the ball, he knocked on and the danger was over. It was a tap-tackle that undoubtedly saved the match for England. Up in the stands the French head coach, Bernard Laporte, could be seen with his head in his hands. He knew how significant that missed chance could prove.

'I saw that the French had four to five players on the other side of the pitch, and then I saw the kick coming so I was on my bike,' Worsley explained later. 'I knew how fast Clerc is, but I just got a bit of his leg. Matches as tight as this one, I suppose, can change on moments like this.' He could not have been more correct. 'I was over the moon I could help out and make a difference,' he added. 'He would have won any foot race against me so my only chance was to knock him off balance. Even then, I had to get on my bike just to touch him.'

'Jonny's got such a world-class head on him'

Martin Corry

Lawrence Dallaglio, Toby Flood and Peter Richards charged on from the bench to replace Easter, Mike Catt and Andy Gomarsall with ten minutes to go. With the game entering its final phase, both of these desperately tired sides knew the next score could well settle it. And so it came. Robinson, once more, probed the French defence inside the 22 and when Szarzewski misjudged the full back's body position, as so many had done so often before, he felled him with a high tackle. Wilkinson made no mistake from in front of the posts and England were back in a lead they first held in the second minute of the game. 'When I got the ball there was nothing on,' Robinson explained later. 'It was just a case of having a go and getting us a bit closer to the posts and, fortunately, it was a high tackle. There was no maliciousness in it, but it put us in a position to go in front.'

The drama was not quite over, though. It took a combination of Flood and Paul Sackey to halt a rampaging Chabal in full flight. The sight of the long-haired, bearded giant being bundled into touch was an uplifting moment for the English players. The fact that he then threw a punch in frustration was almost a badge of honour for Messrs Flood and Sackey. From their next attack Peter Richards spun the ball back to Wilkinson and this time, from 40 metres out, his high, looping, left-footed drop goal found its target and France ran out of time to answer back.

'Jonny's got such a world-class head on him,' said Martin Corry, referring to this moment. 'He's calm. He's calling the shots. He's called the drop-goal routine, so we had to make sure we gave him the ball he wanted. You call it a routine, but it's more that we know the position where Wilko needs it to have a shot. We want to get as close to the posts as possible to give him the best shot.'

Referee Jonathan Kaplan blew for time, the English jumped for joy and the French slumped in despair. 'All the determination and

> ### 'We have a lot of regrets but you have to turn the page otherwise it will haunt you. But the adventure is over'
>
> *Sébastien Chabal*

all the sweat comes to a halt,' sobbed an inconsolable Chabal. 'We have a lot of regrets but you have to turn the page otherwise it will haunt you. But the adventure is over.' For the French, yes, but not for England.

An emotional Phil Vickery paid tribute to Wilkinson immediately afterwards. 'If you had to put your mortgage on anyone, then Jonny's your man,' he said, shaking his head in disbelief that his England team had reached the World Cup final for the second successive tournament. 'He took that penalty and the drop-goal chance as if it was a stroll in the park on a Sunday afternoon. He really is a great kicker.'

Yet Vickery was quick to recognise England were a team full of heroes that night, none more so than Joe Worsley, whose tap-tackle on Vincent Clerc when clean through saved the game. 'It was try time,' he admitted. 'Joe's the kind of player who always gives it a hundred and ten per cent and it is moments like that tackle that are the difference between winning and losing World Cup semi-finals.'

He also spoke of his great friend and colleague at Wasps, Raphaël Ibanez, whose dream of leading out his beloved France in the World Cup final had just been extinguished by Vickery's England. 'I texted Raphaël after France lost their opening game to Argentina and told him I was feeling for him. He texted me after South Africa thrashed us and told me to be strong. We didn't get in touch this week because we both had to focus on beating each other, but I've just seen him and asked if he was OK. I know how much it would have meant to Raphaël to take France to the World Cup final. For England, though, it's a very special day. The underdog has once more risen and come through. It's a magical thing, the World Cup. There's always a twist in the tale somewhere. Sport sometimes doesn't make any sense at all.'

An exuberant Wilkinson was quick, as ever, to praise his team-mates for keeping him going despite his misses that night. 'I get as many opportunities as I do because the guys keep giving them to me,' he insisted. 'Every kick I miss, they get me another one. With a bunch of guys like that, you can't get disheartened. We knew that if we could keep ourselves going with determination we could give it a shot. We were under huge pressure from the French team. They were awesome. Their kicking and tackles were strong and they seemed to have twenty players out there. But events like tonight come from being among a fabulous group of guys. They worked and worked until they were literally almost fit to drop. I can't remember a tougher contest, physically. When I was injured, and out for all those months and years, I guess thoughts of nights like these kept me going.'

Changing the ball did not appear to faze him. 'It's just one of those things,' he explained. 'It's been a challenge. A couple missed, a couple went over and, thankfully, it was in the right order to make it work for us. Rugby at this level is all about getting a shot at the end.' The shot came, and Wilkinson duly delivered.

Listening to Wilkinson was Mike Ford, the England defence coach. His admiration for his stand off was immense after seeing him play against the French. 'I've never worked with anyone like Jonny,' Ford said. 'His reading of the defensive game is pheno-menal. He is everywhere, absolutely everywhere. We all talked about the edge being one player, one pass, one kick or, in our case, one tackle by Joe Worsley. We knew it would go down to the wire. We were even prepared for extra time at one point.'

Brian Ashton must have thought the game was up after that thrashing by South Africa, but here he was as a head coach in charge of the World Cup finalists. 'It's been four cup finals in four weeks and we've won them all,' he said. 'The players deserve mas-sive credit. They've shown incredible mental strength. That's why

'It's difficult to describe how disappointed we are'

Raphaël Ibanez

I selected the squad I did. I knew we needed players who have been here before and were up for the challenge. It's been up and down since I got the job in January, but this is the first time I've had the players together for a long period of time and at last it's beginning to show.'

The head coach was also keen to point out how England kept finishing their games the stronger of the two teams. 'In the last two weeks we've been up against world-class opposition and in both games we've come through strongly at the end,' Ashton said. 'Both times we've been down on the scoreboard and it shows a lot of mental strength to hold the game together. Today was another example of that, against the host country on their home pitch in that sort of emotional cauldron. We talked before the game about how controlling our emotions on the pitch would probably lead to winning the game and I think that probably in the last ten to fifteen minutes we did that better than France did.'

As for his captain, the head coach could not speak highly enough. 'For a prop forward he thinks pretty deeply about what he is going to say,' Ashton explained. 'And he always comes up with the right thing. He made a very moving speech to the squad about seven o'clock on Friday evening. It was only five minutes long. It was about what it meant to him to be playing against France in a World Cup semi-final on their own ground, and what it should mean to everyone else in the room. You saw from the game that it obviously had some sort of effect. Phil is my ideal sort of captain.'

Vickery's friend, Raphaël Ibanez, could not quite believe his side had lost, especially as their passage to the semi-finals had been as dramatic as England's. 'The game was so close and it could have gone either way, but England deserved to win because they took their chances. It's difficult to describe how disappointed we are.'

'If we had scored that try we would have won, but we didn't'

Bernard Laporte

French coach Bernard Laporte knew how important that Worsley tackle on Clerc had been. 'If we had scored that try we would have won, but we didn't,' he lamented. 'Semi-finals always come down to little things. That one came down to nothing. It is all the more disappointing because, while England were better than us in the semi-final four years ago, this time it was fifty-fifty. We wanted to be world champions and now we will not be, at least for another four years.'

His French rugby president, Bernard Lapasset, summed up the Wilkinson factor perfectly. 'The last ten minutes of the match were sealed by one man who does what others can't: Jonny.'

Yannick Jauzion, the man whose try did for New Zealand the week before, could not believe that they had been beaten by this English performance. 'England did not do a great deal against us,' he complained. 'They just waited.' His scrum half, though, Jean-Baptiste Elissalde, was a little more realistic. 'We simply ran out of gas,' he said. 'The match against the All Blacks cost us a lot of energy and we suffered, notably in the rucks. We have the bitter feeling of leaving the business unfinished.'

Nobody would have felt more bitter than Damien Traille, whose slip allowed Lewsey to snaffle the ball and score inside eighty seconds. 'I slipped as I went for the ball,' Traille confirmed. 'We had most of the ball and lost.'

Back in the English camp, everyone was caught up in their astonishing comeback from the dead in this tournament. 'It's a very proud day for English people and it's important we now go and take the next step,' was Dallaglio's take on the night's proceedings. 'We've come here without expectation and we have grown as a team and built momentum. We've reacted well to the pressure we've been put under in adversity. It has brought us together as a squad and we have delivered when it's mattered,

'We'll have a few beers tonight, just as we did after beating Australia last week'

George Chuter

when the pressure was really on. A lot of players in the group are used to playing under huge pressure and in the big games, and you need that. Experience is what you need to take the right approach into these games. France tried to wind down the clock with ten minutes to go and that is a dangerous thing to do against us. We knew we could work our way into a position to score and there is no one better under pressure than Jonny Wilkinson.'

His team-mate at Wasps, Simon Shaw, outlined how the squad's mentality had changed since the last time they had played at the Stade de France. 'I went out for the South Africa game almost with my head down,' he admitted. 'I was just trying to do my job and not look at the bigger picture. It was the same for a lot of us, but the meeting afterwards sorted everything out. We're now much more positive.'

His partner in the second row, Ben Kay, was about to become, if selected, only the second lock forward in history, alongside Australian John Eales, to appear in two World Cup finals. 'We felt the need, after the 36-0 defeat by South Africa in the pool, that we had to prove this team have bottle,' he explained. 'This win against the French, on French soil, means more than our victory over them in the semi-final four years ago.'

George Chuter, Kay's Leicester Tigers team-mate, admitted to be completely taken aback by England's advance. 'To be honest, I'm still in shock,' he said. 'To be in the World Cup final is a bit surreal. Everyone had written us off. We'll have a few beers tonight, just as we did after beating Australia last week, but our focus will swiftly be on the final.'

For Jason Robinson, his fairy-tale career was about to have a fairy-tale ending. Having already retired from club rugby the previous May with Sale, the World Cup was always going to be his last

'Four weeks ago we were a shambles against South Africa. We were written off by everyone'

Mike Catt

hurrah, but now it would be in a World Cup final. 'Who would have thought it?' he asked, not unreasonably. 'I said from day one there were good performances to come from this team and that there were great players in our squad, and I was proved right, first in Marseille last week, and now here in Paris. From the incredible pressure kicking of Jonny Wilkinson to the tackle by Toby Flood and Paul Sackey on Sébastien Chabal, right through to Joe Worsley's stretch and tap-tackle at the end, this was a team effort. It wasn't about individuals.'

Mike Catt, the man who gloriously punted the ball into the Sydney stands four years ago to denote the end of the 2003 World Cup final, had helped his adopted country back into another one. 'It's an absolutely awesome feeling,' he confirmed. 'It's incredible that this England side now finds itself in a World Cup final for the second time on the trot. Four weeks ago we were a shambles against South Africa. We were written off by everyone. Even two weeks ago we were being written off. Now it might be time to take us seriously. I have to mention our defence. It was quite immense throughout. That was what won us the game, as much as anything else. Everyone put their bodies on the line and it won its reward.'

Even so, Catt had to make a special mention of the man whose late penalty and drop goal won the day. 'I said to him before the start that this was Jonny Wilkinson's time,' he added. 'When the chips are down, the man stands up. It is just absolutely brilliant. It is why he is who he is.'

Corry, who had been so lucid over Wilkinson's drop goal, had vowed four years previously, when he felt like an undeserving bit-part player in the World Cup-winning squad, that in 2007 he would be playing a major part. His promise had been kept. Even so, he could not quite believe he would be playing in a World Cup final. 'When you look at it all, after the games against the USA and South Africa compared to now, the feeling we have is disbelief,' he said. 'I've just called the wife and she couldn't believe it, either. She told me she was waiting to be transported back from the parallel universe we seem to be in. It's just brilliant.'

> 'They played a different style to how I thought they would, kicking the ball rather than running with it'
>
> *Lewis Moody*

His club colleague, Lewis Moody, spoke of his surprise at France's tactics. 'They played a different style to how I thought they would, kicking the ball rather than running with it,' he explained. 'With the players they have and the speed and skill of their back division, coupled with their offloading ability, I was sure they would test us a lot more but they never looked like scoring a try, apart from that chance for Clerc. It was not the prettiest game because we did not play as we wanted to, but ours was winning rugby. It feels surreal to be in the final and it is a phenomenal achievement when you consider where we were not that long ago.'

Eight weeks earlier, Toby Flood had to deal with the desperate news that he had not made the final cut for the England World Cup squad. Now he had just come off a semi-final field as a winner. 'The older boys were thinking: "I might never do this again," and the younger boys were thinking: "I might never do this again so I might as well give it a bash."' Flood also revealed why his celebrations were relatively muted compared to his colleagues. 'I wanted to show my respect for my Newcastle team-mate, Jamie Noon,' he explained. 'I only got my chance because Jamie was injured and had to return home. I'm sure, deep down, he has mixed feelings tonight and I didn't want to make things any worse

173

for him. He's trained hard for eight years. He missed out on the last World Cup and now he has lost out on this one, too. The mark of the man is that he rings me up and asks how things are going and he'll be over the moon for us. But I just feel devastated for him, even though behind closed doors I'm delighted.'

On the Sunday night, the England team sat down to watch the second semi-final with interest. Argentina had, in many ways, shared equal billing with England in terms of being the team of the tournament. Without either a Tri-Nations or Six Nations to play each year, their players, nearly all based in Europe, have to make do with 'friendly' tours. But in France, where they were given a shop window, the Pumas made it undeniably clear that they deserved to be treated alongside the so-called giants of the game. They had beaten France at the Stade de France in the opening game of the World Cup; they had dismissed the highly fancied Irish with contemptuous ease; they had seen off a determined Scotland in the quarter-finals.

But South Africa proved too strong for them and ran away with the game to finish up 37-13 winners. It seemed to be written in the stars. England would have a second crack at the Springboks in the World Cup final. Surely they could not produce the greatest turnaround in sporting history and beat a team who had smashed them so comprehensively just a few weeks previously?

It would be the ending to end all endings after a quite ludicrous story and no one quite believed it could happen. No one, that is, except the England squad. And that was all that mattered.

Chapter 8: The Final – England v South Africa

Saturday 20 October at the Stade de France, Paris   *Attendance* 80,000

ENGLAND 6		SOUTH AFRICA 15
Robinson	**15**	Montgomery
Sackey	**14**	Pietersen
Tait	**13**	Fourie
Catt	**12**	Steyn
Cueto	**11**	Habana
Wilkinson	**10**	James
Gomarsall	**9**	Du Preez
Sheridan	**1**	Du Randt
Regan	**2**	Smit (Captain)
(Captain) Vickery	**3**	Van der Linde
Shaw	**4**	Bakkies Botha
Kay	**5**	Matfield
Corry	**6**	Burger
Moody	**7**	Smith
Easter	**8**	Rossouw

Replacements

Stevens (for Vickery) 41 mins
Hipkiss (for Robinson) 47 mins
Flood (for Catt) 51 mins
Chuter (for Regan) 63 mins
Worsley (for Moody) 63 mins
Dallaglio (for Easter) 65 mins
Richards (for Worsley) 71 mins

Du Plessis (for Smit) 72–7 mins
Van Heerden (for Rossouw) 72 mins

Referee   A.Rolland (Ireland)

Scorers

England	South Africa
Wilkinson (penalty) 13 mins	Montgomery (penalty) 7 mins
Wilkinson (penalty) 44 mins	Montgomery (penalty) 16 mins
	Montgomery (penalty) 40 mins
	Montgomery (penalty) 51 mins
	Steyn (penalty) 62 mins

Match statistics

England		South Africa
0	Tries	0
0	Conversions	0
2 (2)	Penalties	5 (6)
0	Drop goals	0
5	Scrums won	9
1	Scrums lost	0
19	Lineouts won	13
7	Lineouts lost	0
4	Turnovers won	4
77	Tackles made	81
11	Tackles missed	16
1	Line breaks	1
55%	Possession	45%
57%	Territory	43%
6'48"	Time in oppo 22	3'22"
10	Errors	8
44	Possession kicked	48
7	Penalties conceded	5
0	Yellow cards	0
0	Red cards	0

England v South Africa Record

Overall	Played 29	England won 12	South Africa won 16	Drawn 1
World Cup	Played 4	England won 1	South Africa won 3	

While the Sunday following England's semi-final win was spent basking in the glow of unexpected success, for one player the day ended in abject misery. Scans at a Paris hospital that morning confirmed that the injury Josh Lewsey sustained towards the end of the first half against France was a torn hamstring. This meant he was ruled out of all rugby for at least three weeks. The try-scoring hero of the semi-final, who had played every single minute of England's World Cup campaign until he limped off the night before, would thus miss out on the World Cup final. England had options to replace him with either Mathew Tait, who could switch to the wing with Dan Hipkiss coming in at centre, or Mark Cueto.

Lewsey had been lucky enough to be part of the starting XV that won the World Cup four years previously, but this failed to lighten his despondent mood. 'Missing the final feels like having a knife through my heart,' he confessed. 'I'm absolutely gutted. Having spent the last four years working to get into this position, I now have to accept I will be watching the final from the stands. I injured my leg when I took the ball from Jason Robinson and accelerated. I knew straight away that my hamstring had gone, even before I was tackled. All I could hope was that the pain was coming from a spasm or cramp, but the medical scan showed a significant tear. Having carried the baton this far, I know someone will take over and, hopefully, get us over the line first. This isn't a time for self-pity and I will be doing whatever I can to help the guys prepare for this match. Ultimately, it has been our mental toughness that has got us this far, having been

> ‘Missing the final feels like having a knife through my heart’
>
> *Josh Lewsey*

written off after the defeat by South Africa in the pool match. Our players know how to win the big trophies and it gives you the ability to bring a calm perspective to moments of real pressure.

'We started way back in June in our old military fatigues with the Royal Marines and I'm certainly not going home yet. All I care about is an England win. I don't care how or why. All that matters is England beating South Africa. Nobody outside the staunchest fan would have bet on England getting to the final. It was nice being written off, because it put us in the luxurious position where nobody expected anything. We've had four good wins, but South Africa are smoking. They are favourites, and deservedly so. They will fancy their chances but you write England off at your peril.'

That humiliation by the Springboks would now be put to good use, according to Lawrence Dallaglio. 'There are no mental scars from that match,' he insisted. 'It was disappointing to watch that happen, but the response has been magnificent. What South Africa did to us taught us all a very valuable lesson and we had to sharpen up our act. After all, we were staring down the barrel. You have seen how we have responded and we have a real chance on Saturday. We've produced performances which the other sides didn't see coming. Remember, in a World Cup you don't necessarily have to be the best side in the world. You've just got to be able to beat the next side. That's what we'll be trying to do against South Africa.'

England's response to the criticisms had been in keeping with the attitudes so many of their personnel. Four years previously, the team reached their peak in time for the World Cup. This time, England really were a motley crew and several of the key figures had defied sporting convention to be here in Paris. Three had already retired once from international rugby: Jason Robinson was lured back by Brian Ashton; Lawrence Dallaglio rediscovered his zest for Test match rugby; while Mark Regan was positively gagging to play again once Ashton was appointed head coach, and told him so in no uncertain terms in a telephone call.

Others had defied the medics to be back playing: Phil Vickery was all but given up for dead by English rugby at one point; Mike Catt had only just recovered from a serious hamstring problem; Lewis Moody had suffered from numerous injuries; and Jonny Wilkinson had bounced back so often that no injury, no matter how serious, seemed to stop him.

Then there were those World Cup winners whose form had fallen away in the interim: Ben Kay was at one point even failing to make the Leicester starting XV; Andy Gomarsall was definitely another, a man who turned from a pub team to the England team in fourteen months. In the case of Nick Easter, a career marauding through Rosslyn Park, Orrell and Rotherham had finally borne fruit with Harlequins, just in time for France 2007. In short, this set of England players were the comeback boys playing in the biggest comeback team in the World Cup.

Nobody was more aware of this than South Africa who, sensibly, were refusing to read too much into the result when the two teams met in the pool stages. Since then the Springboks had enjoyed an easy route to the final, dismissing Fiji with unexpected difficulty in the quarter-final and then Argentina in the semi-final. They expected a much sterner test against England in the final.

'The one thing about England is that they always play with a lot of character,' said Jake White, South Africa's head coach. 'It will be a whole different ball game on Saturday. I think it will be tough. They have a lot of players who were there in 2003, so that's an advantage at the final. The pool stage win counts for nothing when you play in a World Cup final. France have been dominated by

> 'The pool stage win counts for nothing when you play in a World Cup final'
>
> *Jake White*

New Zealand in recent times and ended up beating them here in the quarter-final, so each match must be viewed on an individual basis.'

His captain, John Smit, agreed. 'England have played some good World Cup rugby and that's why they're here,' said the man who watched François Pienaar lift the Webb Ellis Trophy back in 1995 and dreamt that, one day, he would follow suit. 'What happened in the group stages will have no relevance on the final, except that it will motivate England.'

Goal-kicker Percy Montgomery, another experienced old hand, was also keen to build up England. 'They played a great game against France,' he said. 'With Jonny being back, and with some of

'Jonny's still a worry'

Eddie Jones

their other senior players, it means they are a completely different team to the one we played before. They have got a few World Cup winners in their team which gives them composure, so it will be a big challenge for us. It's going to be a really physical battle.'

In short, it was the kind of contest their big lock forward, Bakkies Botha, relished, but he was also aware of the English threat. 'No team gets to a World Cup final without a good reason, so it is going to be tough for us this weekend. I am looking forward to it. We're confident, but England have pulled it around to beat Australia and France. Jonny will get them playing on the front foot as well, but we'll be ready for them.'

The name Jonny Wilkinson kept on being repeated by just about every member of the South African playing and management squad. 'Jonny's still a worry,' admitted Eddie Jones, who saw Wilkinson kick England to World Cup final victory over his Australian side in 2003. 'He's probably not as dominant a player as he was in 2003, but the thing about Jonny is that he gives the England squad enormous confidence and he's still a good player defensively. You can see that guys just play better because he's out there. He has won a World Cup, he kicks reasonably well and he drops a field goal here and there. And he's tough, as he showed with his tackles against Australia and France. You don't go down that channel easily and that forces you to go a little bit wider.'

Two other key players also spoke of the threat from England's fly half. 'Jonny makes a huge difference when he is directing the play,' insisted Fourie du Preez, the best scrum half in the tournament. 'Just his presence gives the guys around him a lot of confidence, so we will have to be aware of that.' The Springbok centre, François Steyn, was another admirer. 'Jonny's a key factor,' he said. 'His drop goals are perfect. He brings a calmness to their team.'

From their perspective, the man England feared most of all was the Springbok flying winger Bryan Habana, whose two semi-final tries against Argentina brought him level with Jonah Lomu on eight tries in one World Cup tournament. 'Our target is to get under twenty mistakes in the final,' revealed defence coach Mike Ford. 'We made only eight in the semi-final. They were our best ever defensive stats, not in terms of tackles made but in terms of making the right decisions within the system. Turnovers can be lethal, especially if you're facing someone as devastating as Habana. In a World Cup final we're going to need a world-class performance.'

Ernie Els, the South African golfer, had attached himself to the Springboks by now. Having won the World Matchplay golf championship at Wentworth on the Sunday afternoon he flew into Paris to watch his beloved South Africa beat Argentina in the semi-final, and then stayed on to talk to the team. He vowed he would also be at the Stade de France for the final. 'It was good to see Ernie and have him on board,' Jake White added. 'He did not make an official speech, but it was nice to see him chat to the younger players. He's such an inspiration to them in the way he has come through to become one of the top golfers in the world.'

White, of course, had the English to thank for saving his job

'Who would have thought we'd reach the final without having to play New Zealand, Australia or France?'

Jake White

after South Africa's win at Twickenham prevented his dismissal, though the same match ended up costing England head coach Andy Robinson his job. He admitted: 'There was a vote of no-confidence, but all I know is that after that there were more votes for me than against me. There's no doubt that performance at Twickenham will help us prepare for the game this weekend. It just proves how close things are in international sport.

'Let's be honest, everyone thought New Zealand were the favourites and France are hosting it, so they would be among the favourites, too. People thought we had a chance but didn't believe we could actually win it. Now they are saying all we have to do is pitch up at the weekend and win the trophy. I find that odd because those same guys probably didn't think we'd beat England in the pool game. Everything has changed. Who would have thought we'd reach the final without having to play New Zealand, Australia or France? It's incredible.'

Almost as incredible as England reaching the final to play against the team that humiliated them in the group, a point the England management were keen to remind their players about. 'South Africa have hammered us in the last three games and we are very aware of that,' underlined forwards coach John Wells. 'You only have to add up the scores. We were frustrated last time at not getting a performance out, because we knew it was in there. Something clicked in their heads that day against Samoa, made them strive that much harder, and that self-belief took them through. Perhaps in hindsight the right game came at the right time. We keep referring as a squad to a specific period during the Samoa match. We were 25-22 up and being battered on our line, but we came out of it with a try when it could easily have gone the other way. We all looked at each other and we knew that was the defining moment of our campaign.'

To complete the job in the final would be a truly remarkable feat, even more than winning the World Cup first time round in 2003. That was certainly Ben Kay's belief, and as he played four years ago and was expected to be named in Brian Ashton's final XV the following day, he should know. 'If we beat the Springboks it will be without doubt a greater achievement,' said the only England player to have played in every single minute of the tournament. 'It will mean more to me than the last time for the simple reason of the trough we've been through as a team and which I've also been through personally. When we won in 2003, the overwhelming feeling among the boys was of a sense of relief. We'd gone into the tournament as hot favourites, didn't play that well and just got home. But to arrive here with everyone telling us we were no-hopers, and to be told we were no good right up until a couple of weeks ago, then to pull it off would be a phenomenal achievement.'

To do so would probably mean winning the lineout, no small challenge when up against Victor Matfield and Bakkies Botha, described by England scrummaging coach Graham Rowntree as 'a right bloody handful'. Furthermore, this time Kay would not be able to crack their code. 'I learnt one to ten in Afrikaans to work out their lineout calls in 2003,' he explained. 'Unfortunately, one of the England management from that 2003 side, vision coach Dr Sherylle Calder, is now with the Springboks. I'm sure she would have told them, so it'll be no use.'

Instead he spent much of the Monday and Tuesday studying DVDs of the South African lineout. 'The codes don't have much to do with it these days,' he said. 'It's more to do with body movements. You have to read that, look for clues and react. South Africa are different from most European teams. There's not a lot of movement going on. They rely on the throw and the athleticism of the jumper. You have to do your preparation and then respond on the day.'

Wednesday, at 1.45 p.m., was the day and the time when all the England players wanted to know whether they would be starting in the World Cup final. After their heroics against France in the semi-final, there were unlikely to be many changes, except for the enforced one in the back three. In what proved to be a close call, Mark Cueto won the selectors' nod to be reinstated on the wing in a like-for-like replacement for Josh Lewsey. The other fourteen players were those who started the semi-final, which left Dan Hipkiss, so close to making the starting XV, on the bench. Toby Flood also retained his place as one of England's seven reserves, so there was no place for Andy Farrell in the World Cup final squad.

For Cueto, who had endured a disappointing World Cup, it was the chance to extend his three-year, and three-Test sequence of never failing to score against South Africa. In two of those occasions the Sale Shark was in direct opposition to Bryan Habana. 'Sometimes you are lucky against certain teams, and going into the final with that record gives me a lot of extra confidence,' a delighted Cueto said in response to his call-up. 'I've got a point to prove in terms of my personal performance, to myself, to my family, friends, everyone. The World Cup hasn't gone exactly as I would have liked. Now I'm just raring to get out there and show people what I can do. We're in a one-off game. Anything can happen.'

Was he happier to be playing back on the wing than at full back? 'I'd have played front row if they asked me,' he replied.

The last Test try Cueto had scored was against South Africa back in November 2006, when England's defeat cost Andy Robinson his job. Ironically, as it would later turn out, that try in a losing cause should not have been awarded because he seemed to lose control of the ball as he touched down. Coming into the tournament, he still owned an impressive strike rate of 13 tries in 20 Tests. Still, Cueto was acutely aware that the final would be a

'To know what true Test match rugby is like, you have to play against South Africa'

Phil Vickery

good time to add to his collection. 'I'm due a try because it's been a while since the last one,' he admitted. 'To get the chance on such a massive occasion as the World Cup final makes it extra special. I played in three of the four pool games, but it wasn't until the knockout stages that we've shown our true character and ability. Unfortunately, I got injured in the Tonga game, then missed out against Australia. After that, it was difficult to change a winning team until Josh got injured. We're mates off the field and I said to him: "I'm sorry for what's happened," but that's sport for you.'

Head coach Brian Ashton had been criticised in some quarters for tinkering too much with the England squad, but for the final he opted for a straight swap on the wing, rather than moving Tait to the wing, thus maintaining the Mike Catt–Mathew Tait midfield axis that fared so well against the French. 'It was a pretty close call, but we decided to stick with the centre combination which got us to the final,' he explained. 'Mark has played a lot of Test rugby in the back three and we expect a fair old aerial bombardment in that area.'

The centre partners were both setting new records: Catt became the oldest man ever to line up in a World Cup final, aged thirty-six; while Tait, at twenty-one, was the youngest England player ever to play for his country in the final.

Captain Phil Vickery was in no doubt that South Africa presented the biggest challenge of England's rollercoaster World Cup campaign. 'It's a scary thing to look at their team, their experience, their power and their speed,' he admitted. 'They seem to have a very complete side, they have been together for a long time and it's very difficult to find any weaknesses. To know what true Test match rugby is like, you have to play against South Africa. For us to rely on the experience of four years ago would be a pretty scary place to go. Experience is fantastic, if used properly. As one of the more experienced players, I know what it took the last time, and if it hadn't been for Jonny Wilkinson we still wouldn't have done it.'

Vickery's ban for tripping an American centre meant he missed out on facing the Springboks in the 36-0 pool defeat, but the pain that night was felt by all. 'We'd like to be able to erase the memories of that 36-0 defeat but, unfortunately, they won't go away,' he added. 'A huge amount has changed since then, but it certainly still hurts a lot of people in the squad.'

Another high-profile absentee that night was Jonny Wilkinson, which explains why so many of the Springboks had been talking about him. England had not lost a World Cup game with the Newcastle Falcon playing for eight years, but still the talisman put himself through the mental wringer. 'I don't think I've ever played in a game when my heart wasn't racing,' he confessed. 'It's been like that since I was eighteen, but that's the life of a goal-kicker for you. People might not think I look nervous – but the reality is different. I'm struggling to enjoy this occasion, but I'm enjoying being here on this fantastic adventure with a fantastic group of players. Four years since the last World Cup has allowed me to step out of the obsessive bubble I was in, take a broader view and get a little more control over my emotions. Then, when Friday comes around, I realise nothing much has changed. For instance, I won't leave the training ground until I'm perfectly happy with my kicking no matter how long it takes. You are desperate to do well for your team. That feeling doesn't change.

'South Africa are leading the way physically in a very intelligent fashion. It's all about wearing the opposition down. We will need to have our brains switched on for every minute on Saturday. That said, the intensity generated within the camp shows that there is nothing more important to this group of players than winning this game. The weight of expectation

'Habana needs the ball before he can do anything ... But, yes, it could be a lively evening'

Paul Sackey

within the squad has never wavered.'

Paul Sackey was as good an example as any of how far this England squad had come on in such little time. Always regarded as a strong finisher, the man who left London Irish for Wasps in search of trophies was thought to have had a suspect commitment, and an even more suspect defence. Sébastien Chabal, having been hit by Sackey in the dying minutes of the semi-final, knows differently.

'A couple of seasons ago I took the criticism on board,' Sackey admitted. 'I might look pretty laid-back, but I work really hard on my game and I'm ambitious. Defensively, Shaun Edwards at Wasps has been a huge influence with just the passion and know-how he puts into your game. I've worked on all the technical stuff defensively, but what I really learnt was that you need to be aggressive and positive going into a tackle. It has been pretty satisfying doing the job well recently. There is much more to being a wing than running in tries.'

He would have to prove it on the Saturday night, because facing him would be Bryan Habana, and he had got the better of almost everyone who had marked him so far in the World Cup. 'He's a great player,' Sackey conceded. 'But South Africa have got a few great players. Habana needs the ball before he can do anything and as a team we have to ensure that we own the ball. But, yes, it could be a lively evening.'

Sackey was no slouch, either, although his journey to the final had taken some time. Opportunities were limited at Wasps, his first club in his junior years, but he struck up a friendship with Andy Gomarsall, and when the scrum half moved to Bedford he arranged a contract for the promising wing. 'I owe Andy a lot,' Sackey said. 'He really looked after me as a young player. He put a good word in for me at Bedford and even arranged my first boot contract. They were good days at Bedford and I've been delighted for Andy to see him play so well in the World Cup and be such an inspirational player for us.

'Bedford was good, but once I decided to concentrate on rugby and not football I was always very ambitious. That's why I moved on to London Irish and then to Wasps. That ambition continues. I always look to the next challenge. When I got into the England team, I wanted to score tries and win. When I got into the World Cup squad, I wanted to start. And now I am in the World Cup final lining up against Habana. If I stop to think too much about it I could become very nervous, but actually it's been a steady progression. I thought perhaps I was getting near to an England breakthrough back in 2001, when I toured North America with Clive Woodward's squad, but it didn't happen. I have had to work even harder for longer, and that might be good in the long run.'

It was a sign of how far England had ventured in this incredible tournament that the likes of Martin Corry were no longer talking in terms of survival, as he was back in the pool stages, and even before the quarter-final, but now in terms of becoming world champions. It was as if all the negatives from that humiliating memory of that pool game thrashing had been erased. Now only positives appeared to be addressed by the England players.

'It's been a great ride but it will count for absolutely nothing unless we continue the journey,' Corry confirmed. 'We've managed, belatedly, to do ourselves justice as defending world champions, but now it's all about us. We're doing this purely for ourselves. It's ironic that you spend your life dreaming about playing in a World Cup final, and when you get there you make yourself underplay it so that you can keep your mind focused. My real emotions will only come out after the game. We're in a cocoon in this hotel, so although you get a bit of a flavour as to what's happening from the television, you can just get on with getting yourself right for the game. We've got to be right on top of

'You've got people coming out of the woodwork wanting tickets, every man and his dog texting you'

Jason Robinson

our game. That's what we're aiming for. It's been great, but we don't want it to stop here.'

Another of England's senior players was also trying his hardest to shut everything out, except preparing for the final, but Jason Robinson, who scored England's only try in the 2003 World Cup final, was finding it difficult. 'I'd be lying if I said I hadn't been thinking back to scoring that try in Sydney,' he admitted. 'It felt good. Winning a World Cup final is the best feeling there is in the sport. But I've also lost a Rugby League World Cup final, and it can also be the worst feeling. You've got people coming out of the woodwork wanting tickets, every man and his dog texting you, and it would be easy to get carried away with it all. You've got to draw it all in a bit because your mind needs to be on the job. This week is all about controlling your thought processes.'

It would prove to be a difficult process for Robinson, who found the thought of a 9 p.m. kick-off not to his liking. 'It's just too late,' he explained. 'I don't mind it when I'm at home and I can get down to breakfast without getting stopped for my autograph. But what can you do here? You're in your room, prowling around, up and down, up and down. You're supposed to sleep during the day, but I can't do that. I can't eat properly, either, so I have to make do with a liquid diet of protein shakes. You're only happy when you can start to switch on.'

For Robinson, it was to be for the very last time. After sixteen years playing first for Wigan and Great Britain, and then for Sale, England and the Lions, the World Cup final – save for a run-out for the Barbarians against South Africa in December – would be his last hurrah. 'It's strange,' he said. 'I've been on the treadmill for so long, yet I won't know what it's like to come off it until next week.

'I know what a fantastic job this squad of players has done'

Brian Ashton

I just can't go there. It's all about one last push.'

The country had certainly taken to the England team's cause. Just as in 2003, England was in danger of slowing to a standstill come Saturday night. Many thousands were making the journey over to France, either to attend the match or just soak up the atmosphere in Paris. All 25,000 Eurostar seats were snapped up in no time, and the city authorities were telling people to bring a tent if they intended to stay in the French capital, with all 75,000 hotel rooms taken.

Messages of goodwill were flying in from all kinds of people. James Bond, in the form of actor Daniel Craig, was one. Prime Minister Gordon Brown was another, although he did admit the removal of Scotland in the quarter-final had made his support of the English a great deal easier. Brown's message included a quotation from Winston Churchill: 'Courage is rightly esteemed the first of human qualities, because it is the quality which guarantees all others.' The Queen, too, sent her best wishes.

'It is fantastic for the players to receive messages from the Prime Minister, the Queen, the England football and cricket teams, and individuals like Daniel Craig,' Brian Ashton proclaimed. 'Daniel's a massive England rugby fan. He sent a message before the semi-final asking for his best wishes to be passed to the team, and now he's phoned through another message from Lithuania where he's filming. "Sorry I can't be there," it said. "Good luck and here's to the cup coming home."

'The fact that we are here is a massive surprise to everyone around the world apart from the guys in the squad. I don't care what anyone says about England, because I know what a fantastic job this squad of players has done. I understand the magnitude of the occasion. I'm not nervous, but then I don't have to go out and play. One or two players might be thinking: "This is my last game for England – what a way to go out." They will all be determined to go out with a bang.'

It was a view reinforced by Phil Vickery in his final message to his troops. On the eve of the final, he reiterated his mantra that getting there was not enough. 'This has been a fantastic journey and now we are very close to the ultimate objective. We have achieved a lot of things which a lot of people didn't expect us to achieve, but being here is not good enough. We do not want to be going home without the cup. We came here with one mission in mind – to retain the trophy. We are under no illusion about the size of the task. Four weeks ago, we were staring down the barrel of a gun and going home if we lost another match. The desire and the will is there from the players to perform at the level necessary if we are to beat as complete a team as South Africa. We all trust each other to get the job done.'

After a day as long as Jason Robinson had predicted, the England team left their hotel and made the short journey to the northern suburbs of Paris. The Stade de France was well on its way to becoming capacity full, with 50,000 of the 80,000 crowd supporting England, when Vickery gave his final address to a bunch of men who had served him so well. 'We have earned the right to be here,' he told his players as a hush descended on the England dressing room. 'We have earned the right to do something which nobody has ever done before. Let's do ourselves proud, and let's make our country proud.'

It was quite a scene as the two teams, led by their respective captains, Vickery and John Smit, walked solemnly out through the players' tunnel, past the glittering Webb Ellis Trophy, and on to the pitch to receive their national anthems and then do battle. The England players made a point of hugging each other and uttering some final words of inspiration. They seemed nothing like the same team that had begun the tournament in such disarray. Theirs had been a triumph over adversity, and even though few shared their belief that night, no player in white imagined losing the World Cup final. The anthems finished, the flash bulbs sparkled all around the stadium and, accompanied by a huge roar, Jonny Wilkinson drop-kicked the ball into play.

Saturday 20 October proved to be a game too far for England's heroic players. Nobody could ever fault their effort or their bravery, but in the suburb of St Denis England's unlikely World Cup dream finally died. South Africa did what others had failed to do in this extraordinary tournament and defeated the team who dubbed themselves 'The Grumpy Old Men'. Maybe they were of limited flair and style, but they possessed unbreakable spirit and this alone ensured that they ran South Africa very close. It was not to be quite enough, though, and the sweet chariot could travel no further.

In defeat, a team humiliated 36-0 by the same Springbok opposition just thirty-six days earlier could hold their heads high and stick out their chests. They had journeyed so much further than anyone had dared to believe and, in the final, with so many decisions and events going against them, England had every justification to feel hard done by. A Mark Cueto 'try' was ruled out in the forty-third minute by the television match official. Phil Vickery, Jason Robinson and Mike Catt all failed to last the distance, and the penalty that sent the Springboks two scores clear was given for the most questionable of offences. There is no doubt that it was a game England could, rather than should, have won, but it is with such fine margins that World Cups are won and lost.

They began the final, as throughout the whole tournament, as rank outsiders. Regardless of their shock wins over Australia and France in the quarter- and semi-finals, the facts were very clear: four defeats in their past four games by the Springboks, a scoreline of 149-32 in the last three, a World Cup try count of 33 to 12 in South Africa's favour, and that 36-0 hammering in the pool game.

Even getting here represented one of the great sporting comebacks of all time. England, after all, had been read the last rites after their previous meeting with South Africa, and rightly so.

Yet, after playing what they described as 'four cup finals' just to get to the Stade de France on World Cup final night, no one in the squad was satisfied with that. They all knew they had not lived up to their world champions label but, in the cold chill of an autumn night in Paris, they had the chance to continue to put things right.

They started well enough, smashing the Springboks in the first scrum and enjoying the early possession, but it was South Africa who took the lead when Mathew Tait slipped in front of his own posts and then failed to release, presenting Percy Montgomery with a simple, seventh-minute penalty. Montgomery had been the best kicker in the whole tournament, Wilkinson included, and he was not going to miss a chance like this to give his side the early lead. In Tait's defence, François Steyn appeared to be all over the outside centre on the floor, which meant Tait could hardly have released even if he had tried. It was a decision that could have gone either way.

Six minutes later, England levelled after Bryan Habana was penalised for not rolling away and Wilkinson found his target, despite the acute angle from the corner. Montgomery then nudged South Africa back into a three-point lead after Lewis Moody had tripped Butch James to concede another penalty. Still, there was plenty of cause for encouragement. At this stage, five weeks previously, the game was already lost, but that was an England side without the suspended Vickery and, perhaps more crucially, the injured Wilkinson. This was an England side with four successive wins under its belt (the best run since the previous World Cup), and with a new-found attitude and approach. They presented a different and much stiffer proposition for the confident Springboks.

Despite some early lineout failures, England were beginning to edge the set-pieces and creating territorial advantage. It was only unforced errors that had handed South Africa the lead, but they already knew, unlike the last time, that they were in a game of rugby. This realisation seemed to jerk them into a big, final ten minutes of the first half. Captain John Smit fell centimetres short of bulldozing over after a scintillating break by the precocious centre Steyn. Then, after a period of sustained pressure encamped on the English line, Montgomery converted a penalty on the half-time whistle to stretch his side's lead to 9-3.

England emerged from their dressing room without their captain. Vickery had twice been attended to by the doctors on the pitch before the break, so it was little surprise to see Matt Stevens on the pitch and itching to have another crack at his former countrymen. Within three minutes of the re-start, high drama hit the World Cup final. A stunning, 45-metre break from the magnificent Tait beat three South African defenders. Weaving and jinking his way from the halfway line, it looked at one point as if the twenty-one-year-old was on the verge of scoring one of the most outstanding tries ever witnessed in a World Cup final, but it was not to be. Victor Matfield, the big South African lock – who would enjoy a stupendous, man of the match-winning game for the Springboks – just managed to bring him down a few metres from the tryline. Quick English ball, however, with the South African defence seemingly struggling, saw Wilkinson flick on to Mark Cueto, who appeared to have dived over in the corner for a try.

The Irish referee, Alain Rolland, turned to the TV match official, Stuart Dickinson, and asked him, in time-honoured fashion, if there was any reason why he should not allow the try. The Australian took repeated views of the tape from at least four angles. The wait seemed like an eternity as the English players stood on the field, their hands on hips, and gazed up at the big screen replaying the move. As Cueto touched the ball down, his left foot was up in the air; but, crucially, moments earlier it had just slid an inch or two on to the touchline and thus out of play after South Africa No. 8 Danie Rossouw's last-ditch tackle. The first

'The least that try decision should have merited was a sin-binning for Mr Burger'

Lawrence Dallaglio

three angles on the replayed footage suggested the try was good. Each time they were played the English contingent in the crowd roared their approval. The fourth angle produced doubt, which only grew the more times it was replayed.

It took three minutes before the final decision was made, three minutes that may well have decided the fate of the World Cup final. The try was refused and Cueto appeared stunned by the decision. Although Wilkinson went on to convert the penalty that had already been awarded for Schalk Burger killing the ball, cutting the arrears to 9-6, there was a sense among the huge contingent of English fans that their side had just been robbed. We will never know, of course, what might have been. The conversion would have been from the corner, and possibly missed as a result, so England might have gained just two points more than the three they seized through Wilkinson's successful penalty, and would still have been a point down, but the momentum gained by the try could have made a priceless difference. England also felt that Burger was lucky to get away without being yellow-carded. 'Those are big decisions that have to be made,' Lawrence Dallaglio observed later. 'We got three points, they got away with fifteen men. The least that try decision should have merited was a sin-binning for Mr Burger. He slid in from about ten metres to kill it and did a very successful job. It was a big decision. We only got three points out of it and that wasn't enough.'

Instead, worse luck was to befall England. Jason Robinson shuffled off injured in the forty-seventh minute, holding his shoulder, and Dan Hipkiss came off the bench and slotted into the midfield, with Tait moving to full back. Robinson would go to a Paris hospital for a scan after the match.

Moments later, Mike Catt left the fray with an injured calf,

'I had not foreseen my career ending in such desolation'

Jason Robinson

with Toby Flood replacing him. In a matter of seconds, England had seen two of their greatest servants in modern times leave the international field for the last time, and with them went 126 caps-worth of experience. 'I had not foreseen my career ending in such desolation,' Robinson admitted afterwards. 'I felt like crying. It was the loneliest walk I can remember. I would have said I was walking away from the game without any regrets – until then.' The fact that he left the field to a rousing reception from a crowd witnessing his last ever performance for England could not have made it any easier.

In between those two injuries, Martin Corry was penalised for hands in the ruck and the tournament's top scorer, Montgomery, slotted home the penalty. It was now looking ominous for England.

Flood quickly made his presence felt when, in a chase with Montgomery for Andy Gomarsall's teasing chip, he ended up pushing the Springbok full back through an advertising hoarding and on to a TV cameraman. The collision looked horrendous, but Montgomery gingerly picked himself up. Flood apologised profusely, and escaped with just a warning from referee Rolland.

Just past the hour, South Africa were awarded a penalty against Ben Kay for crossing, a decision by Rolland that was hard to fathom. Up stepped Steyn with his trademark big boot to launch the resulting penalty kick through the posts. It took some nerve from the twenty-one-year-old, as he calmly smacked the most important penalty kick of his life straight and true. Crucially, the nine-point lead meant England had to score twice to save the game.

On came George Chuter, Joe Worsley and Lawrence Dallaglio for Mark Regan, Lewis Moody and Nick Easter but, within a few minutes, a furious Worsley limped off again with a damaged hamstring. With all England's reserve forwards having been used, Peter Richards, the substitute scrum half, became a flanker in a World Cup final. With luck like this, it became increasingly obvious this was not going to be England's night. Not even this incredible group of players could bounce back from this number of setbacks, and South Africa, who conceded just five penalties all match, allowed the seconds to tick down as they closed out the game until the sweet shrill of the whistle confirmed them as world champions.

Four years previously, a joyous group of English players received their World Cup winners' medals from the Australian Prime Minister, John Howard. Now they knew how the beaten Australians had felt, as they stepped up, one by one, to receive losers' medals from the newly elected French President, Nicolas Sarkozy, while Prime Minister Gordon Brown looked on beside him. Up in the stands, Princes William and Harry, long-time England rugby supporters, held their heads in their hands. They, too, had been in Sydney, and here they were to witness the English flame finally flicker and die. All England's players could do after this was stand and watch as John Smit led his victorious men on to the podium to relieve England of the Webb Ellis Trophy, before celebrating with their President, Thabo Mbeki, who rode high upon the shoulders of the victorious Springboks.

Safely back in the bowels of the stadium, a shattered but magnanimous Phil Vickery was not prepared to make any excuses for England's defeat. 'South Africa deserved their victory and I'm not going to make any excuses,' England's captain insisted. 'We weren't quite good enough. We did not take our opportunities, we weren't clinical enough, and we put ourselves under too much pressure. Everyone's very disappointed because, regardless of what people felt, we believed we really had a chance to win. There were some crucial moments in the game, and some crucial decisions, but we didn't quite have enough on the night. It has been a real rollercoaster of a World Cup for us. We've suffered a barrage of

'You can't fault the effort. You can't fault the effort of everyone'

Martin Corry

criticism – some of it justified, some of it not – but I'm immensely proud to have captained this side, and very honoured to have been part of this adventure. I've played alongside some real warriors.'

One such warrior was England's 'other' World Cup captain, Martin Corry, who was devastated afterwards. 'We've come so far and all the fans have been unbelievable,' said the man who took over the captain's armband in the second half after Vickery failed to re-emerge from the dressing room. 'To be so close and then not to do it is heartbreaking. You can't fault the effort. You can't fault the effort of everyone. It's just a shame when it all counts for nothing. We gave it everything and it's hard to escape an overwhelming sense of dejection and disappointment.' Asked if he felt Cueto's try was good, he replied: 'I don't know. You just have to get on with it.'

Cueto, one hour after the final whistle, was convinced he and England had been wronged. 'You generally have a good feeling straight away when you think you've scored a try,' said the disappointed winger. 'My immediate reaction was that it was a legitimate try, as did eighty thousand other people, and I went straight back to the re-start. I thought you could see from the tape that the ball was grounded well and from the back that I wasn't in touch. For me it was a hundred per cent a try. If Wilko had slotted over the conversion, and nine times out of ten he would have done, then we would have taken the lead. Who knows what might have happened after that? The longer the decision was delayed, the worse it got. Nobody will be able to convince me differently until the day I die.'

Could it have changed the eventual outcome? 'Neither team looked like scoring a try, so it could have won us the game. It's very disappointing but the decision was made and we had to crack on. Afterwards, when I turned on my phone, there were thirty text messages, and twenty-nine of them said we were robbed.'

'It was an absolutely brilliant decision by the television match official'

Paddy O'Brien

Jonny Wilkinson also believed at the time that England had just earned five points. 'It looked OK, but I'm sure the guy making the decision made a good one,' he said. 'Maybe in other games it would have gone our way, but this one didn't. South Africa deserved to win, though. They've been fantastic all tournament.'

Later Paddy O'Brien, the referees' manager for the International Rugby Board, backed Dickinson's decision. 'It was an absolutely brilliant decision by the television match official,' the New Zealander confirmed. 'There is a great photo of Cueto's foot just on the line prior to grounding the ball. There is no issue, there is no doubt. People may criticise officials for taking their time, but it is better that it is correct.'

Dickinson was also adamant he got it right. 'There's no doubt about it,' he said. 'There's stills footage and all the pictures we looked at on the night have been proved to be right. There's a lot of definitive footage there. I'm one hundred per cent happy with the decision. His foot runs into touch. Factually, it is indisputable. Looking at the first replays, it was clear that Mark Cueto had grounded the ball correctly and that his body was in play when he did so, which left the question of whether his toe had slid in as the only issue.'

Lawrence Dallaglio felt that, all night, England had not enjoyed the rub of the green with the match officials. 'We were unlucky with a few other decisions as well as the disallowed try,' he said. 'It was one of those fifty-fifty decisions. If you are an Englishman, it definitely was a try. If you are a South African, it definitely wasn't. On another day, it could have been given but the decisions all went our way in the quarter-final and semi-final.

'The bottom line is that the scoreboard doesn't lie'

Brian Ashton

Today was a day when we needed all the decisions to go our way if we were to win.'

Head coach Brian Ashton was keen to remind people that, with so many promising youngsters waiting for their chance to play Test match rugby, and with others – such as Tait, Flood and Hipkiss – having already tasted a World Cup final, the future for English rugby appeared bright. 'There are a lot of great youngsters as well as many who played tonight,' he said. 'The future's looking good. Right now, though, the only future I'm concerned about is to enjoy tonight with the players and try and put a smile back on their faces. We're bitterly disappointed because we believed we stood a pretty good chance of winning. Congratulations to South Africa. They've been the best team in the tournament, but I'm incredibly proud of my players.' The Cueto try that wasn't did not come into it. 'We had other chances but couldn't take them,' Ashton added. 'The bottom line is that the scoreboard doesn't lie. South Africa won because they took their chances better than we did.'

It was a point a 'gutted' Mike Catt was prepared to concede. 'That game was there for the taking but we failed to do so,' he concluded. 'We had the opportunities but didn't take them. That is what is most annoying about it. We had oodles of pressure, especially in the first half, but could never come away with the points we wanted. The decision concerning Mark Cueto's "try" was mighty close. On such small margins are such important matches usually determined.'

Jake White was keen to pay his respects to England after they had given his Springbok side a thorough challenge. 'England have shown huge character,' said the South African head coach. 'They said they wouldn't give up without a fight and they were true to their word. All credit to them. A lot of people expected them not

'It would have been one of the greatest sports stories of all time'

Phil Vickery

to be as competitive as they were. They were also a bit unlucky not to get a try. Inside I was dying as we waited for the decision and again with five minutes to go. Coming from a country like ours, you only had to see the State President being lifted on to the players' shoulders to know that it doesn't come bigger than that.'

Indeed it does not. For the likes of Phil Vickery and Jason Robinson, Mike Catt and Jonny Wilkinson, World Cup finals had provided the whole gamut of emotions. In 2003 it was sheer ecstasy. In 2007 it was a numbing sensation.

No player had settled for just making the final, incredible achievement though it was. They accepted the fact that, considering the build-up before the tournament, and then their stumbling passage through the group stages, it was a comeback to rank with the great sporting comebacks. But still it was not enough.

'It would have been one of the greatest sports stories of all time,' Phil Vickery pointed out, as he made his way into the night to sink a few well-deserved beers. 'When I look at it like that, it makes me feel very sad.'

In truth Vickery's England team had captured the hearts of the nation. It is one thing going into the tournament as favourites. It is quite another arriving in Paris with no expectation whatsoever. The British public warmed to their heroics, and willed them on to complete a truly remarkable story. They had gone from the brink of almost total capitulation to the brink of ultimate glory, all in the space of thirty-six days. It was a very British story. The fact that they fell at the final hurdle – and only just – does not erase the remarkable feat they achieved during the weeks of September and October. They proved, whatever the formbook says, that anything is possible in sport.

As they headed back to their homes and their families, many

of the more experienced members of the squad felt like losers. They were in a minority. Everyone else saw them as winners. They did not successfully defend their world title, but what Brian Ashton's men achieved in France 2007, under the most extreme of circumstances, was very close to being on an equal footing with their predecessors from four years ago. Defeat, even in a World Cup final, can indeed be glorious.

Conclusion

Name	Club	Date of birth	Caps	World Cup apps	Points
Nick Abendanon	Bath	27/8/86	2	–	0
Olly Barkley	Bath	28/11/81	21	US, S, T	18
Steve Borthwick	Bath	12/10/79	32	SA, S, T	0
Mike Catt	London Irish	17/9/71	75	US, SA, A, F, SA	0
George Chuter	Leicester	9/7/76	19	US, SA, S, T, A, F, SA	0
Martin Corry	Leicester	12/10/73	64	US, SA, S, T, A, F, SA	10
Mark Cueto	Sale	26/12/79	24	US, S, T, SA	0
Lawrence Dallaglio	Wasps	10/8/72	85	US, T, A, F, SA	0
Nick Easter	Harlequins	15/8/78	12	SA, S, T, A, F, SA	0
Andy Farrell	Saracens	30/5/75	8	US, SA, T	5
Toby Flood	Newcastle	8/8/85	12	A, F, SA	0
Perry Freshwater	Perpignan	27/7/73	10	SA, S	0
Andy Gomarsall	Harlequins	24/7/73	33	SA, S, T, A, F, SA	0
Dan Hipkiss	Leicester	4/6/82	6	S, T, F, SA	0
Ben Kay	Leicester	14/12/75	53	US, SA, S, T, A, F, SA	0
Josh Lewsey	Wasps	30/11/76	55	US, SA, S, T, A, F	5
Lee Mears	Bath	5/3/79	18	T	0
Lewis Moody	Leicester	12/6/78	52	US, SA, S, T, A, F, SA	0
Jamie Noon	Newcastle	9/5/79	27	US, SA	0
Shaun Perry	Bristol	4/5/78	14	US, SA	0
Tom Rees	Wasps	11/9/84	8	US, SA	5
Mark Regan	Bristol	28/1/72	43	US, SA, A, F, SA	0
Peter Richards	Gloucester	10/3/78	12	US, SA, T, A, F, SA	0
Jason Robinson	Unattached	30/7/74	51	US, SA, A, F, SA	5
Paul Sackey	Wasps	8/11/79	10	SA, S, T, A, F, SA	20
Simon Shaw	Wasps	1/9/73	43	US, SA, S, A, F, SA	0
Andrew Sheridan	Sale	1/11/79	20	US, SA, S, T, A, F, SA	0

Name	Club	Date of birth	Caps	World Cup apps	Points
Matt Stevens	Bath	1/10/82	21	*US*, SA, S, <u>T</u>, *A*, *F*, *SA*	0
Mathew Tait	Newcastle	6/2/86	19	*US*, *SA*, <u>S</u>, T, A, F, SA	5
Phil Vickery	Wasps	14/3/76	60	<u>US</u>, *T*, <u>A</u>, <u>F</u>, <u>SA</u>	0
Jonny Wilkinson	Newcastle	25/5/79	65	S, T, A, F, SA	67
Joe Worsley	Wasps	14/6/77	65	<u>US</u>, <u>S</u>, *A*, *F*, <u>*SA*</u>	0

Abbreviations: A = Australia, F = France, S = Samoa, SA = South Africa, T = Tonga, US = USA; appearances in *italics* denote substitute appearances, appearances in <u>underlined</u> denote players who were substituted.

The Back-room Team

Brian Ashton	Head coach
John Wells	Assistant coach
Mike Ford	Assistant coach
Jon Callard	Specialist coach
Graham Rowntree	Specialist coach
Viv Brown	Team manager
Simon Kemp	Team doctor
Barney Kenny	Physiotherapist
Phil Pask	Physiotherapist
Calvin Morriss	National fitness coach
Dave Sylvester	Conditioning coach
Matt Lovell	Nutritionist
Richard Wegrzyk	Masseur
Dave Tennison	Kit technician
Richard Prescott	Media manager
Dave Barton	Press officer
Tony Biscombe	Technical support manager
Ross Appleton	Technical support assistant
Richard Smith	Legal advisor

t had been the most extraordinary of World Cups from the very first game – when Argentina had upset hosts France – to the very last, when two teams from the same pool met each other in the final for the first time in the tournament's twenty-year history. Along the way all kinds of dramas unfolded. The pool stages, normally a predictable and often pointless *hors d'oeuvre* in which the big boys embarrass the small nations before the main course takes place, this time served up a feast of veritable treats.

Out went Ireland, beaten by both France and Argentina, and out went Wales too, upset by a rampaging Fiji in what was arguably the game of the whole tournament, in Nantes. The so-called minnows of the World Cup punched way above their weight, from Georgia nearly beating Ireland to Tonga nearly upsetting South Africa. The likes of Samoa, USA, Canada and even Portugal all had their moments, and the debate about whether the number of teams in forthcoming World Cups should be reduced became nonsensical as a result. Any talk of the number of teams now being reduced to sixteen looks ridiculous in light of the 2007 World Cup, and in the case of both Argentina and the three South Pacific Islands, places in major tournaments outside the World Cup now look inevitable.

In the knockout stages, the 2007 World Cup continued in the same vein. France shocked hot favourites New Zealand in a pulsating quarter-final; Fiji almost did the same to South Africa; and Argentina, although favoured to beat Scotland, qualified for their first ever semi-final, where they would fall to the Springboks but end a glorious campaign by defeating the French to finish up in third place.

Yet none of this could compare with England's story. Nothing in the intervening period between the last World Cup and France 2007 hinted that the defending world champions would come so close to becoming the first nation ever to win back-to-back tournaments. They had not even looked like winning a Six Nations title in that time, and they came to France on the back of two demoralising defeats to the World Cup hosts in warm-up Test matches that were designed to provide a clear idea of England's first-choice starting XV, but instead produced more questions than answers.

The lacklustre display against the USA turned out to be the prelude for England's lowest World Cup ebb, the 36-0 humiliation against South Africa in the pool stages. At that point, there was a very serious possibility that either Samoa or Tonga would beat them in the remaining pool games to make the English the worst ever defending world champions.

Much has been said and written about the week immediately following the thrashing by the Springboks before the next game against Samoa. There was no doubt that a set of mitigating circumstances resulted in that South African setback. Captain Phil Vickery was serving the first of his two-match ban, talisman Jonny Wilkinson was out injured. When Olly Barkley, the man of the match against the USA, also fell foul to injury, England had to do with a makeshift stand off and inside centre combination which had no time to gel before such an enormous game.

When Wilkinson returned, against Samoa, he helped himself to 24 points and then a further 16 the following week as England beat Tonga to qualify for the knockout stages. His reinstatement in the team meant a great deal more than just kicking the penalties and conversions, important though this undoubtedly was. Wilkinson's presence, his direction, his drop kicks and his aura, which permeated into the opposition's psyche, made a massive difference; and this, coupled with the return of the hugely influential Vickery from his suspension, took place just in time for the England ship to be steadied.

Yet there is little doubt that the pivotal off-field moment in England's whole World Cup story took place on the Saturday morning after that South African mauling. The four-and-a-half-hour meeting instigated by Brian Ashton and Phil Vickery that took place in the Trianon Palace Hotel, Versailles, was heated and emotional, passionate and at times angry. Some of the Northern Hemisphere's biggest rugby stars had been humiliated by the previous evening's events and it was abundantly clear, on the back of this and the way in which they struggled to dominate the American Eagles the week before, that England stood no chance of keeping hold of the Webb Ellis Trophy at this rate.

It is at times like this when the sport of rugby comes into its own. It requires an honesty that can often hurt, but can also lead to a dramatic renaissance. More and more details of what really went on during this meeting appeared in the media within days of the England players returning to their clubs and their homes after the World Cup had finished. The players were together in their frustrations and made their feelings clear to the management. Head coach Brian Ashton had tried to give as much authority to the players as he could, but the results hadn't worked out as he'd hoped. Some told the head coach to his face that fifteen players had fifteen different ideas of how to play each game. Others, including some senior players, felt so demoralised that they would have quite happily packed their bags and gone home.

But it was the venting and exchange of views that changed everything. On top of that, the coaches were willing to hear what was said and take on board the constructive criticisms and utilise them. A few had previously felt the coaches had not appeared to be in complete harmony themselves concerning tactics and selection, and all agreed this needed to be resolved. This acceptance of the need for change, and the siege mentality that had suddenly become apparent, transformed the squad.

In short, the players and coaches realised that their previous policy had not worked. Beforehand everyone had different opinions and different ideas. At the clubs there are usually two or three senior players who always have their say when it comes to tactics. With England, all these players were assembled in one squad. It led to everyone airing their views on playing styles, and this was encouraged by a management keen to give the players a free rein.

After South Africa, everyone came to the conclusion that they needed to sing from the same hymnsheet. There was no complete change in style, or different game plan, or new direction, but rather everything was simplified so that every player knew exactly what was expected of him. It was only after this meeting that the squad really came together as a collective entity and that every player understood what his role was during the game. It was the fact that all the squad and the management agreed on the same game plan and bought into it that resulted in the remarkable transformation of fortune for England.

The English, as a nation, can be many things, but write them off, tell them they are useless, and have them up against a wall with one last chance to redeem themselves, and they come into their own. It has proved to be just about their most telling characteristic, and it became evident once again in France 2007. The players became galvanised. They bonded better than if they had participated in any organised bonding activity. From the most senior to the junior players in the squad, they were in it together and the players began to work out for themselves how to meet the challenges thrown at them by the World Cup.

It still needed the bounce of the ball and decisions to go their way for England to come through, just as it always does in rugby. Even South Africa could have lost to Tonga in the pool stages, and again against Fiji in the quarter-finals.

In England's case, there came a moment against Samoa when their sizeable lead had been reduced to three points as the Polynesians' second-half surge looked on the verge of causing one of the biggest upsets in the tournament's history, but England dug deep, pulled away and won the day, and from that point onwards, they never looked back.

Of course it was not all plain sailing after that. Tonga took a deserved lead against them in the final pool game, but England, playing with some rediscovered if belated confidence, dealt with the serious question asked of them in emphatic style. They had reached the knockout stages the hard way, but at least they were there, and few had worked out whether Ashton's previous tactics had been an abdication of responsibility or a unique way of giving authority to his players. Either way, it would produce a quarter-final win over Australia that few outside the England camp saw coming.

In hindsight the result makes more sense. England had reached this far by coming through must-win games against Samoa and Tonga. Lose either of them and they would have been out and going home in ignominy. As they would often explain, they had already played two knockout games and this, coupled with their vast experience of pressure matches in Heineken Cup games, as well as title deciders, promotion and relegation issues, stood them in good stead.

Australia, in contrast, had cruised through their group, with only Wales posing any kind of problem at all. They were unprepared for a fight, whereas a battle-hardened England were itching for one. The Wallabies also had a major problem unexposed during the group. Their front five, and especially their front row, were a weak link, and one that England exploited to the full.

By the time the semi-finals came round it was anyone's game. France may have been the favourites by virtue of a partisan home crowd cheering on the tournament hosts; they may have suggested 2007 would finally be their year after eliminating New Zealand in the quarter-final, but France are France. Stifled by head coach Bernard Laporte's strange tactics of employing a kicking game when Les Bleus sported one of the finest back divisions in world rugby, and by the pressure of knowing they were just eighty minutes away from a World Cup final, they crumbled against the streetwise English. Even so, it still came down to fine margins in the guise of a late tap-tackle and an even later penalty and drop goal.

And so to the World Cup final, a game that England stood no chance of reaching a month before, but now entered believing they could win. It would have been up there with Muhammad Ali's rope-a-dope victory over George Foreman to reclaim the heavyweight world title in terms of sporting comebacks if they had pulled it off, but in defeat England still emerged as absolute heroes back home in a country which forgave all group stage sins for the incredible ride the players had given everyone who followed sport.

So what now? At the time of writing, the RFU review is ongoing. Head coach Brian Ashton, whose contract runs out on 31 December, is yet to discover where his future lies. Some players have publicly expressed the view that he is one of the best coaches around, but needs assistance in off-the-field management. As for the players, two have already retired (Jason Robinson and Mike Catt) and others may well have played their final Test for England. Some of the remaining senior players, such as captain Phil Vickery, Jonny Wilkinson and Josh Lewsey, expect to be part of the 2008 Six Nations, while everyone in English rugby is excited by what the future holds for the national team.

Already there is a younger nucleus of players emerging who featured in the 2007 World Cup. The likes of Andrew Sheridan, Matt Stevens, Lewis Moody, Nick Easter, Mark Cueto, Paul Sackey, Toby Flood, Mathew Tait and Dan Hipkiss, alongside Vickery, Wilkinson and Lewsey, expect to be around for a number of years yet.

Then there are the many youngsters who have already tasted international rugby with England. The likes of Shane Geraghty, David Strettle, James Simpson-Daniel, James Haskell, Tom Varndell, Anthony Allen and Olly Morgan are just a few of the many confident young men who are expected to be pushing hard for places in a future England team.

'Now I'll believe anything's possible'

Phil Vickery

By 2011, given a little luck, a lack of injuries, a willingness to back players and adopt a consistent selection policy, and an acceptance that a few defeats in the next year or two may be the price to pay for ultimate glory at the next World Cup in New Zealand, England may well be expecting a third consecutive World Cup final. And next time, they may just go one step further and reclaim the Webb Ellis Trophy they won in 2003, and lost in such dramatic circumstances four years later when an England team that was ridiculed and written off, ashamed and humiliated, suddenly turned on the world and came out fighting.

In truth they were not as good a squad of players as their predecessors from 2003. But in fighting spirit, mental strength and sheer bloody-mindedness not to accept the seemingly inevitable, they are up there with the very best.

The memories of finally winning the Rugby World Cup in 2003 will never fade for those who lived through those seven weeks in Australia. Yet, despite ultimate defeat, England's 2007 Rugby World Cup campaign will be remembered just as strongly, and as fondly, for proving that in sport there is no such thing as a lost cause.

England captain Phil Vickery summed it up best as he looked at his World Cup final loser's medal and then recalled the last few weeks of his life. 'Now I'll believe anything's possible,' he said, as he shook his head in bemusement. 'Sport really can be so very strange.'

Indeed it can, which is why so many millions lived through every ounce of pain, hurt, relief, joy, ecstasy and final disappointment as they followed England complete their unlikely story. It was a journey well worth taking.

Results and Records of the 2007 Rugby World Cup

Pool A

Date	Venue	Result	
8 Sep	Lens	England 28	USA 10
9 Sep	Paris	South Africa 59	Samoa 7
12 Sep	Montpellier	USA 15	Tonga 25
14 Sep	Saint-Denis	England 0	South Africa 36
16 Sep	Montpellier	Samoa 15	Tonga 19
22 Sep	Lens	South Africa 30	Tonga 25
22 Sep	Nantes	England 44	Samoa 22
26 Sep	St-Etienne	Samoa 25	USA 21
28 Sep	Paris	England 36	Tonga 20
30 Sep	Montpellier	South Africa 64	USA 15

Pool A Final Table

	Played	Won	Drawn	Lost	Pts Diff	Tries	Bonus Pts	Points
South Africa	4	4	0	0	142	24	3	19
England	4	3	0	1	20	11	2	14
Tonga	4	2	0	2	-7	9	1	9
Samoa	4	1	0	3	-74	5	1	5
USA	4	0	0	4	-81	7	1	1

Pool B

Date	Venue	Result	
8 Sep	Lyon	Australia 91	Japan 3
9 Sep	Nantes	Wales 42	Canada 17

12 Sep	Toulouse	Japan 31	Fiji 35
15 Sep	Cardiff	Wales 20	Australia 32
16 Sep	Cardiff	Fiji 29	Canada 16
20 Sep	Cardiff	Wales 72	Japan 18
23 Sep	Montpellier	Australia 55	Fiji 12
25 Sep	Bordeaux	Canada 12	Japan 12
29 Sep	Bordeaux	Australia 37	Canada 6
29 Sep	Nantes	Wales 34	Fiji 38

Pool B Final Table

	Played	*Won*	*Drawn*	*Lost*	*Pts Diff*	*Tries*	*Bonus Pts*	*Points*
Australia	4	4	0	0	174	30	4	20
Fiji	4	3	0	1	-22	14	3	15
Wales	4	2	0	2	63	23	4	12
Japan	4	0	1	3	-146	7	1	3
Canada	4	0	1	3	-69	6	0	2

Pool C

Date	*Venue*	*Result*	
8 Sep	Marseille	New Zealand 76	Italy 14
9 Sep	St-Etienne	Scotland 56	Portugal 10
12 Sep	Marseille	Italy 24	Romania 18
15 Sep	Lyon	New Zealand 108	Portugal 13
18 Sep	Edinburgh	Scotland 42	Romania 0
19 Sep	Paris	Italy 31	Portugal 5
23 Sep	Edinburgh	Scotland 0	New Zealand 40
25 Sep	Toulouse	Romania 14	Portugal 10
29 Sep	Toulouse	New Zealand 85	Romania 8
29 Sep	St-Etienne	Scotland 18	Italy 16

Pool C Final Table

	Played	Won	Drawn	Lost	Pts Diff	Tries	Bonus Pts	Points
New Zealand	4	4	0	0	309	46	4	20
Scotland	4	3	0	1	50	14	2	14
Italy	4	2	0	2	-32	8	1	9
Romania	4	1	0	3	-121	5	1	5
Portugal	4	0	0	4	-171	4	1	1

Pool D

Date	Venue	Result	
7 Sep	Saint-Denis	France 12	Argentina 17
9 Sep	Bordeaux	Ireland 32	Namibia 17
11 Sep	Lyon	Argentina 33	Georgia 3
15 Sep	Bordeaux	Ireland 14	Georgia 10
16 Sep	Toulouse	France 87	Namibia 10
21 Sep	Saint-Denis	France 25	Ireland 3
22 Sep	Marseille	Argentina 63	Namibia 3
26 Sep	Lens	Georgia 30	Namibia 0
30 Sep	Marseille	France 64	Georgia 7
30 Sep	Paris	Ireland 15	Argentina 30

Pool D Final Table

	Played	Won	Drawn	Lost	Pts Diff	Tries	Bonus Pts	Points
Argentina	4	4	0	0	110	16	2	18
France	4	3	0	1	188	24	3	15
Ireland	4	2	0	2	64	9	1	9
Georgia	4	1	0	3	-61	5	1	5
Namibia	4	0	0	4	-182	3	0	0

Quarter-finals

Date	Venue	Result	
6 Oct	Marseille	Australia 10	England 12
6 Oct	Cardiff	New Zealand 18	France 20
7 Oct	Marseille	South Africa 37	Fiji 20
7 Oct	Saint-Denis	Argentina 19	Scotland 13

Semi-finals

Date	Venue	Result	
13 Oct	Saint-Denis	England 14	France 9
14 Oct	Saint-Denis	South Africa 37	Argentina 13

Third place play-off

Date	Venue	Result	
19 Oct	Paris	France 10	Argentina 34

Final

Date	Venue	Result	
20 Oct	Saint-Denis	England 6	South Africa 15

Tournament Records

Leading Points-scorers

Percy Montgomery	South Africa	105
Felipe Contepomi	Argentina	91
Jonny Wilkinson	England	67
Nick Evans	New Zealand	50
Jean-Baptiste Elissalde	France	47

Leading Try-scorers

Bryan Habana	South Africa	8
Drew Mitchell	Australia	7
Shane Williams	Wales	6
Doug Howlett	New Zealand	6
Vincent Clerc	France	5
Chris Latham	Australia	5
Joe Rokocoko	New Zealand	5

Paul Sackey was England's leading try-scorer with 4 tries

Leading Points-scorers in Rugby World Cup History

Jonny Wilkinson	England	249
Gavin Hastings	Scotland	227
Michael Lynagh	Australia	195
Grant Fox	New Zealand	170
Andrew Mehrtens	New Zealand	163